RESTING LIGHTLY ON MOTHER EARTH

The Aboriginal Experience in Urban Educational Settings

Angela Ward & Rita Bouvier

Detselig Enterprises Ltd.

Calgary, Alberta, Canada

Resting Lightly on Mother Earth

© 2001 Detselig Enterprises Ltd.

National Library of Canada Cataloguing in Publication Data

Main entry under title:

Resting lightly on Mother Earth

Includes bibliographical references.

ISBN 1-55059-221-1

1. Indigenous peoples–Education–North America. 2. Australian aborigines–Education. 3. Indigenous peoples–Urban residence–North America. 4. Australian aborigines–Urban residence. I. Ward, Angela II. Bouvier, Rita E.

E96.R47   2001   371.829'97   C2001-910596-7

Detselig Enterprises Ltd.

210-1220 Kensington Rd. N.W., Calgary, AB, T2N 3P5

Phone: (403) 283-0900/Fax: (403) 283-6947

E-mail: temeron@telusplanet.net

www.temerondetselig.com

We acknowledge the financial support of the Government of Canada through the Book Publishing Industry Development Program (BPIDP) for our publishing activities.

SAN 115-0324

ISBN 1-55059-221-1

Printed in Canada

Table of Contents

Introduction

Angela Ward (University of Saskatchewan)
Rita Bouvier (Saskatchewan Teachers Federation)

Themes of the Book

Resting Lightly on Mother Earth contributes to the discourse on cross-cultural studies in urban contexts. The chapters in this book illustrate how class differences, access to resources and education differentially shape Aboriginal people's experiences in urban centres. For some, adapting to urban life has meant opportunities for educational advancement and a chance to live and work with a wide range of people from different backgrounds. For others, city living is an unremitting struggle for survival among daily encounters with overt racism. However, there are common struggles: Indigenous peoples, whatever their circumstance, continue the struggle to maintain strong cultural identities as they seek full membership in society. Despite the challenges presented by an environment where relationships are fragmented and impersonal, and where meeting basic needs is sometimes a daily struggle, Indigenous people are certain that their identities were not left at the edge of the city when they arrived in this place and space (Royal Commission on Aboriginal Peoples, 1996). Understanding the context of Aboriginal peoples' experiences in urban centres is crucial to determining the strategies that might be employed through education systems that are devoted to the "public common good."

Identity

The authors of the Royal Commission on Aboriginal Peoples (1996) concluded that the main issues affecting Aboriginal peoples in urban centres are identity, a void of government policy, accessible and appropriate resources, and the gaining of an effective voice in governance and decision making. According to the Royal Commission report, Aboriginal people have become increasingly urbanized, and those who find employment and social acceptance in the city blend into the multicultural surrounding, while those who encounter difficulties retain high visibility, reinforcing the stereotype of Aboriginal people as poor, marginalized and problem ridden. The chapters in this book would concur with this observation; however, they would also invite further exploration of the meaning of "blending in" and the cost to individual and collective identity.

An issue that appears to be of central concern to all Aboriginal people, regardless of their personal circumstance, is that educational strategies must achieve more than "blending in." While the source of who we/Aboriginal people are comes from our/their history, our/their language and culture, it is also shaped by interaction or in relationship with others. Identity is also about who we (Aboriginal people) want to become by "asserting the power we Aboriginal people possess as communities and individuals to make decisions that affect our lives" (Warrior, 1995, p. 124). The importance of history, language and culture to the formation of identity has gained much attention in cross-cultural studies. However, little attention has been given to how identity is shaped by society as it is constructed in relationship with others based on differences of race, class and gender.

Generally there is absence of a discussion about our/their future as Aboriginal people – as Indian, Métis and Inuit – within society. The lack of attention to the latter aspects of identity formation is in part the result of a lack of recognition of the historical relationships with Indigenous peoples worldwide (Martinez, 1998), a lack of recognition that our Aboriginal cultures are changing and evolving as we/they attempt to meet the challenges we/they face in meeting our physical, economic, social and spiritual needs now and for future generations. It also reflects a deeper malaise of a political environment based on race, class and gender that accords full human attributes to some and not to others, and how a failure to realize these differences shape relations and accord power to individuals and groups.

McCarthy (1988) warns us that the broad theoretical sweep of radical scholarship may obliterate the specific struggles and histories of oppressed peoples. Within the educational community, multiculturalism has been proffered as an antidote to the poison of deficit theories. However, this idealistic approach underplays the role of racial domination in the negative school experiences of Aboriginal children. The relations of differential power are not abstract: they support or hinder identifiable groups of real people. As you read the stories of real people in this book, bear in mind the interplay of social forces that have created the backdrop to their daily struggles. Perhaps there is a tendency for us as educators to seek the all-encompassing solution; multicultural approaches to curriculum may be valuable in supporting children's understanding of the rich social fabric of North America, but the writers in this book suggest that social justice goes beyond recognition of existing cultural differences. There is a powerful attraction in acquainting students with the picturesque aspects of exotic cultures, but Kymlicka (1995) suggests that, even for minority groups who have lost some aspects of their societal cultures, "It is the potentiality of societal cultures that matters, not just their current state, and it is even more difficult for outsiders to judge the potentiality of a culture than to judge its current state" (p. 100). Educators working with urban Aboriginal students go beyond multiculturalism and invoke this potentiality when they build coalitions with Aboriginal communities to forge a new sense of what it might mean to be Cree, Dene or Métis, and living within an urban environment.

Disconnection From the Land

The title of the book, *Resting Lightly on Mother Earth*, is a quotation from the chapter by Dottie King, Bill Walters, Sharon Wells and their participants, that explains how artifacts of the North American urban scene, unlike traditional Aboriginal buildings, have been built with apparent disregard for the earth on which they sit. Cities are rootless, temporary constructions disconnected from the natural world. This search for ecological balance is common to many city dwellers. The relationship of human beings to nature changed forever in North America when Europeans mapped, distributed and fenced land.

"In the gathering-hunting economy, Indians, wild animals, plants, and rocks were all face-to-face material subjects in a space-time web" (Merchant, 1989, p. 67). This is a stark contrast to Europeans, who saw the natural world as an enemy to be subdued. Modern cities, with their mechanistic control of the environment, cocoon us all from nature's power. A strong relationship to the land, for survival and spiritual renewal, has been considered a defining characteristic of Indigenous cultures (Hampton, 1995). Moving away from a space that affords more opportunity for a connection to one's natural surroundings may mean the weakening of many cultural dimensions described by Hampton (1995) as crucial to Indian education. Many of these dimensions (or "standards," as Hampton calls them) are affected by urban living. Such dimensions as tradition, which Hampton describes as an affirmation of Indian education through continuity across the generations, or the Indian sense of place, land and territory, are a struggle to maintain identity in disconnected urban environments.

Spirituality is the Key to Understanding Aboriginal World Views

Tradition and continuity have been the cornerstones of North American Aboriginal cultural survival throughout the colonial era (Cajete, 1994; Ermine, 1994). The stories shared by the participants with the researchers in many of the book chapters reinforce the importance of continuing in this tradition. Elders of many groups insist that children must learn their culture through traditional education on the land. A sense of a connectedness to the natural world, as well as to the people in it, is developed through extended experiences on the land, either in company with an elder or alone. Kawagley (1990) suggests that all human beings build knowledge on a blending of pragmatic, inductive and spiritual perspectives. Every culture has established a way to make the natural world accessible to reasoned inquiry. Being in tune with the natural world is a challenge for a generation of Aboriginal people who grew up in the city and whose identity may be framed only through stories, family contacts or visits to the family's place of origin. Still others remember their traditions but may not have the means (both in an educational and an economic sense) to create opportunities to extend their connection to place and to people who might nurture their identity. Those who remember their traditions and have the means to connect with their extended families and places of origin have managed to make sense of their complex lives and extend who are they are in the urban environment.

Dene elders expressed this view of traditional Aboriginal ways of teaching and learning in an account of a series of workshops conducted by Lamothe (1994). The Dehcho people of northern Canada traditionally believed that most children were born with the spirit of someone who has lived before, and so "the work of bringing an individual to full awareness of that knowledge, so that knowledge will benefit the community, becomes one of creating a safe environment where the child will grow in self-confidence and feel comfortable and safe to display what it knows to be good for the community" (p. 36). There are "elder programs" in some urban schools that enrol a high proportion of Aboriginal students, but even students who are fortunate enough to work with traditional elders in a school setting do not experience the extended "tag-along" learning of culture with an older family member to whom they might have access in the home community. The respect for other people and the creation engendered by learning on the land is more difficult to provide for city children. The challenge of the educational system in the future might be an examination of structures and environments for learning that can connect students in a more intimate way to natural surroundings and life.

The Effects of a Colonial Legacy

Beyond the ecological imbalance of city living, writers in this book also deal in some way with the consequences of cultural imperialism. Another common underlying theme, while it is not explicitly stated, is the effect of a colonial legacy. This legacy is the dispossession of land and the slow erosion of languages and cultures through legislation and policy, which resulted in a breakdown of systems that ensured survival as Indigenous people, then and now. It is a legacy that has extended into the hearts and minds of Indigenous peoples, shaping understandings about who they/we were as Indigenous peoples, challenging their/our present efforts to define who they/we are and who they/we might become. As you listen to the voices of young people in this book, particularly those without the means to connect "home," you cannot help but feel empathy for their loss and sometimes warped sense of what it means to be "Indian." This suggests that curricular efforts to integrate Indigenous knowledge and ways of knowing are important to them, as well as to their classmates.

The path to self-determination, a future that has been expressed as a political goal and a goal of social justice by Aboriginal peoples, involves processes of transformation, decolonization, healing and mobilization (Smith, 1999). What is the role of educators in these processes? An obvious role is one of extending their own learning and incorporating what they have learned into their practice, while a less obvious role is one of advocacy for those suffering in the present conditions that affect the development and learning environment of their students. The despair wrought by "oppression of poverty, the oppression of being without work, the oppression of racism and sexism, the oppression of colonization" is immense and its effects need to be better understood. Moving to an urban centre does not remove the burden of a colonial history. Aboriginal people in Canada who have moved from Indian reserves, Métis settlements and Inuit communities to the city may experience further cultural dislocation, economic hardship, discrimination and powerlessness, with disastrous social and political consequences, since the pressures to integrate with mainstream society are more pervasive in the urban milieu, and the resources and structures to support their continued development as Aboriginal people are less evident, if not non-existent (Canada, Royal Commission on Aboriginal Peoples, 1996).

Stories in this Book

Many chapters in this book describe the struggle and strategies for balanced lives as Aboriginal people come to live and work in the cities. The tensions of urbanization, recognized by many who live in cities, are exacerbated for Aboriginal people because they often experience the additional challenges of poverty, unemployment, poor education or racism. The four sections of this book illustrate the range of urban Aboriginal responses to city life. The first section presents a broad overview of experiences of Aboriginal people living in urban areas in Canada and Australia, while the second section describes the experiences of students who are particularly marginalized by poverty, the effects of cultural dislocation and racism. The next section shifts to the identity-affirming work of one particular teacher education program. Finally, the last section describes Aboriginal and non-Aboriginal professional people working together in the city.

The first section of the book, "Intercultural Perspectives," begins by presenting an overview and critique of the literature surrounding Aboriginal peoples' experience in education. It challenges the reader to re-examine the construction of culture through which we might understand the lives of Aboriginal people living in urban environments. In the first chapter of the book, Carol Reid takes a broad look at the experiences of Aboriginal Australian peoples' experiences in urban environments. Reid argues that a colonialist discourse continues to treat Aboriginal students as a homogenous group, concealing differences such as gender, class, age-generation and location. She recognizes that the attending factors affecting the education of Aboriginal students are multifaceted and complex. She argues that traditional explanations of the non-recognition of culture or cultural differences as explanations of underachievement are not sufficient in the urban context, especially against a backdrop of poverty and violence. More importantly, she argues, our construction of culture needs re-examination. Culture as it concerns Indigenous peoples continues to be construed as static, as a deficit or a barrier to learning. Research on learning styles has only shifted the cultural dissonance or deficiency argument to the teacher, she claims. A "culturalist" analysis leads to Aboriginal essentialism that ignores the issue of power – colonization, race and class. This does not negate the importance of a discussion on the role of culture in education, one that holds to a dynamic view of culture and one that views culture as negotiated even in situations where individuals or groups may feel powerless. The students' voices demonstrate that this is a constant process.

Angela Ward shares the struggles she has experienced in her intercultural research involvement, recapitulating the shift from emphasis on cultural difference to activism at the classroom level. She describes her first research experience as an alarmed observer of young Aboriginal children struggling with classroom structures that shut down their possibilities for participation. Subsequent projects enabled Ward to face her own complicity in a system that has prolonged the effects of colonization, while she tentatively built coalitions with Aboriginal and non-Aboriginal educators as they worked together with children in the inner city.

The second section, "Surviving the City: Stories of Identities Lost and Regained," deals with the everyday lives of Aboriginal students and teachers who face difficulties in urban schools beyond those of poverty and substandard living conditions. Rita Bouvier leads off with her vision of good community schools. She suggests that, despite the call for social justice accompanying the foundation of community schools in Saskatchewan, systemic issues of poverty and racism writ large in Canadian society have never been addressed. Policy documents for community schools do not typically acknowledge that the populations they serve are largely Aboriginal, nor are issues of colonization recognized. Bouvier challenges her readers to look beyond cultural difference in order to understand the malaise affecting urban education. The Aboriginal students described in these chapters often meet the challenges of surviving urban schools by demonstrating overt or covert resistance.

Carol Leroy and Heather Blair document different manifestations of students' resistance to school. Blair describes how gender, race and "coolness" played themselves out "in the margins" of students' school experiences. These powerful organizing realities need to be recognized and better understood. Leroy interprets resistance as evidence of urban Aboriginal students' search for belonging. They often have difficulty establishing their cultural identity, which is frequently compounded by poverty, dislocation and uncertainties with one's relationships in the inner city environments. Mismatches between home and school experiences for Aboriginal students have often been described by researchers in terms of cultural differences in learning and communication styles (for example, Philips, 1983). The observations made by the researchers in these articles suggest the need to go beyond cultural differences and communication style. Stairs (1994) suggests that what she terms "cultural negotiation" should occur in cross-cultural classrooms. Stairs describes cultural negotiation as occurring at three levels of awareness, each focusing on specific aspects of schools' adaptation to Indigenous culture. The first focuses on the "what" of Indigenous education, such as the language and cultural content of curricula; the second looks at how communication and language patterns may be adjusted to support learning in a cross-cultural context; the third goes beyond these to think about the cultural values that underpin community life. Stairs makes the point that "School becomes a forum for negotiation among surrounding cultures, between itself and the community" (1994, p. 156).

An example of this cultural negotiation is demonstrated as Linda Wason-Ellam offers an analysis of her classroom observations and teaching, chronicling the struggles and successes in providing culturally appropriate curricula in schools. She poignantly describes the way in which one young Aboriginal girl's everyday stories initially reflected the confusions of her life, but were later enriched by gentle encouragement and an immersion in culturally relevant literature. Cultural negotiation has the potential to enrich classroom life for students whose lives have been relegated to the margins of urban society.

Transformational work can be accomplished at the systemic level and also in the small encounters of our everyday lives in the city. Shauneen Pete-Willett, an Aboriginal storyteller, conceptualizes her consulting role in an urban-based school division as a Coyote story. She weaves a complex tale of her own learning and survival while she attempts to negotiate a meaningful role as an Indian and Métis Education consultant. She is caught "doing Indian" as she attempts to make friends. She discovers the limits of strategies that focus on cultural difference. She models, mentors, weans and acts as a mediator and communication link to outside agencies and Aboriginal organizations. Overwhelmingly, the responsibility for creating change seems to belong to her, as she prods non-Aboriginal colleagues in tiny increments towards a distant view of counter-hegemonic curriculum.

In the third section of the book, "Rebuilding Culture: Teacher Education with Urban Aboriginal Peoples," we move to a different site of struggle, where one particular teacher education program becomes the pathway for cultural regeneration for those who teach and learn there. Bente Huntley recounts her experiences teaching science to Métis and First Nation pre-service teachers. She emphasizes the importance of creating relevance in science by learning from nature rather than about nature, and using the oral tradition and interactive strategies to reinforce learning. She challenges her readers to align their perceptions, their beliefs and their values with the real things that keep us alive. She invites us as educators to pay attention to gender-related issues, which are reinforced daily within the scientific labor market. Finally, she reminds her readers about the important role that children play as they assume responsibility for the earth.

Drama was the heart of Lon Borgerson's work with Aboriginal student teachers in the Saskatchewan Urban Native Teacher Education Program. Improvisation provided a collaborative way of exploring issues affecting the students' lives. The process began with each individual student learning about himself or herself, and then moving into a collective process to learn about and with each other. Through this process, stories of oppression gave way to hope, inspiration and transformation. Improvisation became an integrated method for teaching across subjects. Students developed skills in writing, research and meta-cognition while covering a range of subjects such as history, literature, music, dance and visual arts. Through this process students learned to trust and support each other in their learning.

The final section of the book takes the reader into the lives of Aboriginal and non-Aboriginal professionals who have built intercultural coalitions through their work. "Touching earth in the city" does not provide solutions to the issues raised in the book, but it does offer possibilities of transformation, collaboration and reconciliation. Dottie King, Bill Walters and Sharon Wells bring stories from professional Aboriginal people living in urban environments in the United States. The key question they explore with their participants is how they maintain their Indianness in an urban environment. The professional Aboriginal people they interview for their study see themselves as part of their own communities, even though they are not physically there. With a few exceptions, all plan to return to the reservation to live. They do not express alienation, perhaps because their financial status affords the opportunity to return home to attend special events or to work in organizations that support their continuance as Aboriginal people.

Passing on stories to their children is another strategy to maintain the connection to "home." The urban environment has provided different opportunities for them and many have found a sense of community here. There is, however, a sense of loss in their voices, particularly when they speak about their relationship to the land; as one participant says, "All people can understand the land by living on it and caring for it."

The book closes with reflections from Rita Bouvier and Angela Ward, in which the editors position themselves socially and culturally, and revisit the book's themes from an educational perspective.

References

Cajete, G. A. 1994. *Look to the Mountain: An Ecology of Indigenous Education.* Durango, CO: Kivaki Press.

Canada. 1996. Royal Commission on Aboriginal Peoples. Ottawa: Minister of Supply and Services Canada.

Ermine, W. J. 1994. "Aboriginal Epistemology." In *The Circle Unfolds: First Nations Education in Canada,* edited by M. Battiste and J. Barman, pp. 101-12. Vancouver, BC: University of British Columbia Press.

Hampton, E. 1995. "Redefinition of Indian Education." In *The Circle Unfolds: First Nations Education in Canada,* edited by M. Battiste and J. Barman, pp. 5-46. Vancouver, BC: University of British Columbia Press.

Kawagley, O. 1990. "Yup'ik Ways of Knowing." *Canadian Journal of Native Education* 17, no. 2: 5-17.

Kymlicka, W. 1995. *Multicultural Citizenship.* Oxford: Clarendon Press.

Lamothe, R. (in workshop with Dehcho gah Dene Elders). 1994. *Dene Teaching Methods.* Yellowknife, NWT: Dene Cultural Institute.

McCarthy, C. 1988. "Rethinking Liberal and Radical Perspectives on Racial Inequality in Schooling: Making the Case for Nonsynchrony." *Harvard Educational Review* 58, no. 3: 265-79.

Philips, S. 1983. *The Invisible Culture.* New York, NY: Longman.

Stairs, A. 1994. "Education as a Cultural Activity: Stories of Relationship and Change." *Canadian Journal of Education, 19,* no. 2: 121-27.

Warrior, R. A. 1995. *Tribal Secrets.* Minneapolis, MN: University of Minnesota Press.

Section One

Intercultural Perspectives

Chapter 1
"Magpie" Babies[1]: Urban Aboriginal Students, Identity and Inequality in Education

Carol Reid, University of Western Sydney, New South Wales, Australia

It has been over 30 years since Aboriginal people in Australia were granted citizenship. Indeed, the 1967 referendum was to become one of a number of firsts over the next two decades. Commonwealth government intervention in Aboriginal affairs from that time on brought with it a flurry of activity aimed at bringing long overdue citizenship rights to all groups of Aboriginal people. Broad goals for Aboriginal and Torres Strait Islander education were set at the national level and encompassed pre-school, primary, secondary and tertiary levels. At the same time there was recognition that the states and territories had different needs and therefore different agendas.

New South Wales (NSW), the first state colonized in Australia, has a different demographic profile than the Northern Territory, for example, where some groups still live on their traditional lands. In NSW, processes of colonization had relentlessly herded up people and placed them in reserves with mixed language and cultural groups. Attempted genocide in various locales (Millis, 1994; Goodall, 1996), coupled with the removal of children[2] effectively wiped out many languages and cultures. Over 200 languages and 600 dialects were spoken all over Australia before colonization. The rapid urbanization of NSW[3] affected Aboriginal relationships to land by disrupting traditional trading routes and ceremonial activities. As towns sprang up, Aboriginal people lived on the outskirts, subsisting in tin shelters and on government handouts. For a period, some gained work on farms. During World War II, Aboriginal people who were not enlisted kept farms running for absent men. It was the further removal of land to provide "soldier settler" farms to war veterans, aided by a policy of assimilation, that saw the gradual internal migration of Aboriginal people to large country towns and the metropolitan areas of Sydney.

In rural towns this migration caused conflict. Many attempts to have children educated in white schools were met with hostile responses from white parents, culminating in the development of separate Aboriginal schools (Fletcher, 1989a). During the assimilationist era (up to 1967), most children were gradually incorporated into white schools, but many were given poor treatment, such as placement in slow learners' classes. Cultural difference was seen as cultural deficit on the part of Aboriginal children.

With the post-World War II mass expansion of cities through immigration and internal migration, urban planners designed housing estates with schools and little else. Such suburbs fringed the cities and some larger towns in rural areas. In Sydney, the capital of NSW, the southwest and west of Sydney became large areas of government housing. At the time (the 1960s through to the early 1970s), the Department of Housing's policy of integration meant "pepper-potting" Aboriginal people throughout these dormitory suburbs (Grace et al., 1997, p. 7-11). That is, they were not allowed to settle in clusters, but were dispersed throughout the region. The rationale was that *they* would be more likely to integrate and less likely to cause any problems if *they* were spread around. Such approaches reflected racism and pathologized the behavior of Aboriginal people. While the power of such policies cannot be denied, and their impact upon individuals and families was intense, migration from the country also meant more opportunities, rather than fewer, to communicate with others in a similar situation. It is not mere coincidence that the 1970s saw the birth of Aboriginal organizations, many with their origins in Redfern, an inner urban suburb of Sydney. A period of cultural revival and celebration of survival followed and continues. The Aboriginal Children's Service, the Aboriginal Legal Service and the Aboriginal Medical Service were all established in the 1970s.

However, changes in education had been brewing since the early 1960s, when the NSW Teachers' Federation had disclosed the inequitable state of the Aboriginal schooling system. The Aboriginal Schools Committee was formed in 1961 to investigate Aboriginal education at all schools. The committee advised the government that Aboriginal schools should be abolished due to the conditions on reserves where most schools remained (Fletcher, 1989a, p. 272). The

Teachers' Federation pointed to the link between socio-economic status and educational outcomes.

Of particular interest to this discussion is the historicity of the relationship between difference and inequality in terms of the curriculum, for it reveals some of the tensions in the discourses related to culture and education in the contemporary period. The Assistant Director-General of Education at the Joint Committee on Aborigines, 1965-67, when asked whether teachers needed specialized qualifications, commented:

> *There was originally a curriculum for Aboriginal schools. This went out of existence in the 1940s, and it is a very good thing that it did. The normal primary school curriculum is broad enough to include all the needs of Aboriginal children in those age groups. The same applies to the secondary program. (Fletcher, 1989b, pp. 256-57)*

These comments reflect the assimilationist trajectory during the 1960s and into the 1970s. The ideology continues today in many contemporary discourses about standards, empowerment and difference in education. Finally, the period of debate during this time raised the issue of introducing Aboriginal studies into the general curriculum as a way of developing "self-respect" in secondary and primary schools (Fletcher, 1989b, p. 259). This idea of "self-respect" is central to policy responses today, though it has now become widely known as *self-esteem*. Aboriginal Studies became the vehicle through which Aboriginal identity was constructed in the minds of educators and other children.

This emerged after a struggle over the place of culture in the curriculum. This paralleled a more general debate. The 1970s saw the development of a multiculturalist philosophy in government policy and educational practice in relation to immigrants. This was important since one out of every two people in Australian cities are first and second generation immigrants (Collins, 1991). Space for "culture" had been created, indeed was the product of, a multicultural society. Kalantzis et al. argue that assimilation failed because of the very nature of Australian society, which is and has always been diverse. The combination, then, of a context for change in the general political arena and the centralization of Indigenous affairs, produced opportunities to challenge policies and practices that had made culture invisible. The formation of the National Aboriginal Education Committee in 1976 resulted from the centralization of Aboriginal affairs after the referendum in 1967. It called for the setting up of Aboriginal Education Consultative Groups in each state.

The NSW chapter was formed in 1978 and the first Aboriginal Education Policy in NSW was released in 1982.

This chapter will examine how the Aboriginal Education Policy in NSW attempted to deal with the relationship between culture and education, particularly in relation to urban students. The emergence of *self-esteem* in Aboriginal education policy reflects not only the way in which culture is understood but also the centrality of the discourse of individualism. The argument is that earlier frameworks focused on culture as something that was fixed and largely based upon ethnicity-as-culture (Keeffe, 1992). These interpretations of "culture" have presented a number of paradoxes for teachers and students. After a discussion of the policy I will attempt to explore what is the most complex part of teacher student relationships in the contemporary period – that of identity. To explicate this process I will draw on the voices of Aboriginal students in a high school in southwestern Sydney.

Constructing Aboriginality and Curriculum Discourse

The *Aboriginal Education Policy*, 1982, was a watershed in Aboriginal education in New South Wales (NSW). In all, there were five booklets covering the Policy Statement, Guidelines for Teaching Aboriginal Studies, Strategies for Teaching Aboriginal Students, the Effects of Culture Contact on Aboriginal People and Resources in Aboriginal Studies. "The policy had two purposes: to enhance the development and learning of Aboriginal students; and to enable all students to have some knowledge, understanding and appreciation of Aboriginals and their cultural heritage" (Aboriginal Education Policy, 1982, p. 5). The strength of the documents was that they mobilized teachers because of the detail and clarity of the documents.

One of the central elements of the policy was the involvement of community, which I came to appreciate as a new teacher working in an inner city school with a high number of Aboriginal students in 1982. Over the next few years, through developing our own school-based Aboriginal Studies policy and curriculum, I met with many parents and community members. These were not always easy times, but provided opportunities for negotiating through conflict the presuppositions of our cultural differences. I recall a situation that provided me with my first sense of the complexity of the issues of identity. I and a group of teachers from my school attended a meeting in the home of one of the Aboriginal parents. We were all sitting around trying to find some common ground. There was clear discomfort. The parents had many concerns and were outlining a number of matters that gave them concern about the education of their children. At some point, a senior male member of the group gave an example of how the children are turned off school.

> *My granddaughter come home the other day all upset that she got into trouble for not doing her homework. She likes school, my grand-daughter, but she's starting breaking out in a rash and I'm having trouble getting her to school. Now she wants to change schools. We can't have her doing that. Now what makes me angry, is that there's too much pressure placed on these kiddies. What is happening to her to make her come out in a rash?*

Something familiar clicked in the story. I asked the child's name. I said I was her teacher. We sat opposite each other and I explained, in the face of his anger, that I simply thought she was bright and wanted to encourage her and that I didn't realize I was pressuring her. To this he responded, "No, don't stop encouraging her, we just have to let her know that is what you are doing and we have to ease off a bit, work together on this one." We negotiated further the way in which the culture of the school needed to take account of the culture of the home.

The First of its Kind (Wammara Aboriginal Centre, 1992), an evaluation of the Aboriginal Education Policy, makes three interesting points. Firstly, despite increased retention of Aboriginal students in Australian schools, the retention rate is still only 50 percent of that of non-Aboriginal students. Secondly, "Aboriginal students perceive that they are coping less well with their studies than non-Aboriginal students" (p. 5, point 6 and 8). Thirdly, "school staff believe that they have been successful in increasing Aboriginal students' self-esteem" (p. 5, point 10).

The first is important because it is a measure of the success of programs implemented during the 80s and 90s (*National Review of Education for Aboriginal and Torres Straits Islander Peoples*, 1995). On the other hand, it points to continuing inequity in terms of educational outcomes and subsequent access to the labor market. Statistical data revealed that speaking English – rather than an Indigenous language – living in an urban area and being female, seemed to be among the factors that indicated greater chance of retention and success (*ibid.*, p. 71). The urban/rural/isolated and gender differences are critical not only to understanding the quantitative data about these issues, but also in breaking down the colonialist discourse that treats Aboriginal students as belonging to a homogenous culture. One of the key points of the 1982 policy was that Aboriginal *cultures* were to be recognized and local communities involved to prevent this homogenization. Yet despite this, explanations are based on Aboriginality; that is, through the rubric of ethnicity-as-culture (Keeffe, 1992). Ethnicity-as-culture conceals differences such as gender, class, age and location. The significance of deconstructing these categories is illustrated by the next two points that seek to arrive at some sort of explanation for this phenomenon.

The second point, that "Aboriginal students perceive that they are coping less well with their studies than non-Aboriginal students," leads us into an altogether different area of tackling the issue of inequality. The National Review of Education calls for some qualitative research to tell us more about the basis for continuing inequities and to attempt to explain how we might overcome them structurally and in terms of classroom practice. Some research has attempted to do just that through ethnographic studies focusing on the micropolitics of the classroom (Malin, 1990). Studies have pointed to the low expectations of teachers, culture-clash, differences in learning styles and racism as factors contributing to unequal outcomes. In these wide-ranging studies there has been an attempt to deal with the production of cultural space in schools. The outcome for practice has often been to focus on issues of self-esteem, to make students feel more comfortable in the classroom and to acknowledge culture. As a focus for practice, self-esteem strategies provide ways in which teachers can gain a sense of agency in sometimes very constraining work environments. It is not surprising then that we find that "school staff believe that they have been successful in increasing Aboriginal students' self-esteem." This is revealing, for it reflects the convergence of policy with hegemonic individualism. The positioning of the voices of the students in the second point has altogether different interpretations about self-esteem and its relationship to inequality.

The common conflation of achievement with self-esteem – that is, the assumption that low achieving students (e.g., minorities) have low self-esteem – appears rejected in this instance. Griffiths (1993) argues that because of this conflation, action has centred on unconditional regard and redefinement of attainment. In practice this has meant unlearning helplessness and curriculum perspectives and broad-based assessment profiling achievements. This has led to stereotyping such as "black kids being good at dance and sport," while at the same time rejecting the real politics of identity that are grounded in experiences of belonging and not belonging. Connections don't fit as easily as universalizing categories suggest: "one's identity is not a set of characteristics which one shares with others of the same identity, but rather is a shared experience of exclusion in oppressive societies" (Griffiths, 1993, p. 308).

One of the traditional explanations for Aboriginal student underachievement in schooling is that there is non-recognition of culture or cultural differences. When this is set against another discourse that explains the relationship between crime, poverty and violence as a consequence of "lost" culture, we end up with a powerful dependence on particular constructions of culture. We need to understand these issues a little more so we can understand what we mean by the urban context and therefore notions of inequality and identity.

What are the Dimensions of Culture in an Urban Context?

In *Mainly Urban: A Report into the Needs of Urban Dwelling Aboriginal and Torres Strait Islander People* (1992), the NSW Aboriginal Education Consultative Committee stated:

> *The cultural isolation of most Aboriginal people in urban and especially metropolitan centres is further aggravated by the fact that many of these Aboriginal people lack the support of family and kinship network....(p. 193)*

This quotation highlights the ways in which urban Aboriginal people are deemed to have "lost" their culture, indicated by the anthropological term "kinship." While assimilationist policies of the past sought to do this, we need a much more dynamic model of "culture" to understand the way in which Aboriginal adolescents negotiate their identity in the context of schooling in highly urbanized spaces. We need to understand the generational changes and impact of policy and other forms of popular culture. Cultural renewal has been a strategy to deal with "re-establishing the pride and dignity of Aboriginal people, and thus their capacity to participate in society as equals with non-Aboriginals" (*Mainly Urban*, 1992, p. 192). Given the high priority placed on the development of "self-esteem" – and its vehicle "culture" – as having the potential to create equitable outcomes, it becomes necessary to define, firstly, the way in which culture is understood.

Marcia Langton (1981), an Aboriginal academic, has argued that "urbanizing" Aborigines is a myth of social scientists. This she argues is because of a static concept of culture and a reification of "traditional" culture. Framed in this way, culture is seen as separate from education and therefore constituted as a "thing" that could be passed around more or less intact and outside of education. Part of the reason anti-racists in Britain have rejected multiculturalism is due to this conception of culture in education (Troyna et al., 1992). Such approaches have led to a kind of solipsism that would have us trapped in our own little homogenous worlds, remaining a mystery to each other (Fay, 1996, p. 10). This is, of course, one of the "unintended consequences of an overwhelming emphasis on cultural difference" (Keeffe, 1992, p. 100). This is because there is a conflation of multiple meanings of cultural difference into one based only upon "ethnicity" (*ibid.*). Culture becomes a set of practices, meanings and "inherited social relations" (Morris and Cowlishaw, 1997, p. 5). From this perspective, culture has become an impediment to "Other" knowledge.

Cultural difference is still seen as an impediment by those who hold the common sense or racist view that everyone should be treated the same and should assimilate. However, unsettling this perspective is another view that sees certain forms of cultural difference as worth celebrating. At its most simple level there is the celebration of dance, dialect, dress and diet (Daniels, 1986). In this view, cultural difference is not a hindrance but something to be celebrated and/or consumed. Cultural tourism is an example of a growth area working within the construction of culture-as-a-resource.

"Culture" is used as a resource in the development of state-funded positions in schools, colleges and universities. Part of the rationale for employing Indigenous people in designated positions is to draw upon their knowledge of Indigenous culture/s (*National Aboriginal and Torres Strait Islander Education Policy*, 1989, 1.2.7, 1.2.8;). Indigenous personnel are also meant to change attitudes, provide input into curriculum development and to act as a conduit between communities and institutions (Wammarra Aboriginal Education Centre, 1992, Vol. 1).

One of the consequences of seeing culture-as-a-resource is that instead of changing student behavior and practices (as in the impediment approach), teachers now have to cater to a range of learning styles. Some of the features of this paradigm suggest that cultural incompatibility is the source of inequality (Lipka, 1990) because Indigenous people have different "world-views." This anthropological notion of culture is concerned with "embedded practices and meanings" which create a sense of common identity (Morris and Cowlishaw, 1997, p. 3). The argument here is that Indigenous students have different ways of learning from non-Indigenous students because of these commonalities. The teacher has merely to harness these learning styles by incorporating cultural differences such as specific socio-linguistic forms of expression and social organization of the classroom for the student to succeed. While the "Other's" culture is a resource (Indigenous), the "Other" culture (the teacher's) is an impediment.

Cultural dissonance is still the underlying problem and explanation for educational inequality, but now the teachers have to change, not the students. Culture is co-opted and incorporated to achieve cultural compatibility. This paradigm has much in common with the "cultural maintenance" paradigm of multiculturalism (Kalantzis et al., 1990). Culture, then, slides "on a continuum of meaning from culture-as-a-thing to culture-as-a-process" (Keeffe, 1992, p. 9).

There are a number of critiques of the culturalist model, or what I have called the culture-as-a-resource model. They stem mainly from the fact that differences embodied by the "Other" are made to seem natural, as if they arise from some sort of essential Aboriginality. There are numerous examples of this theoretical paradigm from Indigenous and non-Indigenous academics. This is a central concern for critical theorists who have argued against the development of so-called "learning styles" theory. The logic of learning styles theory is centred around dualisms that are a "seemingly neutral scapegoat" (Nicholls et al., 1996, p. 6) in explaining educational inequality. Keeffe (1992) cogently argues that this concern for ethnic absolutism "ignores the vexed questions of the powerlessness and inequality of social groups in favour of explorations into the sources of their identity" (Keeffe, 1992, p. 81).

If we focus on the general logic of current frameworks that attempt to explain inequality in Indigenous education, we can place them into what Connell defined in *Gender and Power* (1987) as extrinsic and intrinsic accounts. The most common extrinsic or systemic theory is that of "culture clash." Here we have the well-documented innate differences between all Indigenous and all non-Indigenous people. The general logic suggests that because non-Indigenous teachers are more individualistic, competitive and future oriented, they will not be able to understand and cater to their students. This is because Indigenous students are group-oriented, non-competitive and present oriented. The usefulness of this theory, in terms of highlighting cultural differences, is offset by the way in which culture is presented as static and homogenous.

In the above models, "social structure is constantly reproduced rather than constantly constituted" (Connell, 1987, p. 44). At the psycho-social level we have a range of intrinsic theories, one of which is a focus on custom. Custom or learned behavior is translated here into teaching and learning styles. The difference between learning-styles theory and the notion of culture clash is that one is socially rather than biologically constituted.

Learning styles theory has had a powerful impact in all areas of education, but particularly in Indigenous education. Indigenous students, it has been argued, learn better in situations that are practical, hands-on and group-oriented. This theory has been useful in that it has been the basis for a politics of reform. However, it constitutes a kind of social determinism whereby teachers are at risk of defining and constraining student options through a range of stereotypical expectations. Of course this is the essential paradox of liberalism, that it "tolerates diversity only as an instrumental quality and not as something valuable in itself" (Griffiths, 1993, p. 309). The ultimate outcome is truth and uniformity.

So we need to hold on to a dynamic model of culture that recognizes agency within constraints. In urban spaces that are ravaged by the fiscal policies of contemporary times, we must attend to this process so that the Aboriginal adolescent's cultural milieu can then be understood, not in terms of what it lacks, but in terms of how it is negotiated. The next section will listen to the voices of some students to demonstrate this process and to explore what this means in relation to the issue of self-esteem.

Self-esteem and the Production of Culture

Stuart Hall (1996) argues that "identities are about questions of using the resources of history, language and culture in the process of becoming rather than being: not 'who we are' or 'where we came from,' so much as what we might become, how we have been represented and how that bears on how we might represent ourselves" (p. 4). When talking to students in our original study, we found that the process of self-identification was often expressed as a conscious process of creation.

I think its good [being Aboriginal]. I go and find out about me past relatives and that. I found out all different things about them. It's pretty good. [male]

It is during the process of reconstruction, which is part of the Aboriginal Studies course, that students come to understand what it has meant to be Aboriginal for other generations.

My Dad's Mum, his Mum's mother, she lives down in [suburb] and she was taken away from the family because she is Aboriginal...that is where he was going to get his information from, because she knows heaps. But she wouldn't tell him because she doesn't want to talk about it. [female, 16]

This type of knowledge has a number of effects. One is the identification, particularly among the female students, with other Aboriginal people in the area:

...all the Aboriginal families that live around in the area, you may as well say all support each other and help each other and they...all get jealous because they don't support each other. (female)

This is a process of authentication that reflects a sense of belonging/not belonging that demonstrates the "fundamental importance of relationship rather than achievement in forming a self" (Griffiths, 1993, p. 311). The self-discovery of belonging while not wanting to belong is powerfully related to historical connections:

I go home, to all me relos [relatives] on the mission there. They get out Charlie Pride and sing. (male)

But the reality of living in marginal suburbs, which are underresourced and lacking in employment opportunities, means that the visibility of Aboriginal people often brings with it a heightened sense of exclusion/inclusion.

You want to be proud of it [Aboriginality] all the time but sometimes you can't be...well sometimes you see all the black fellas laying over there and they say, Ah, you're going to be like that because they're related to you. [male]

This recognition of a political reality means that the problem of self-respect, the basis of self-esteem activities, must include recognition of this politics of identity because the juxtaposition of this reality with "book Aboriginality" does not escape the students. A discussion about Aboriginal Studies and who should teach it reflected the way in which power operates in schooling. The students were adamant that teachers had to respect their identity and be open.

I don't like it when they say we go 'walkabout' when we're not in class. [male]

"Walkabout" was, and sometimes still is, a rite of passage for Aboriginal males. It is an initiation into adulthood and occurs during adolescence. However, it is often used in a negative sense to portray Aboriginal people as inconsistent, lazy wanderers. This term, borrowed from more traditional contexts, reflects a slippage from "book Aboriginality" to a dynamic urban context. The subtleties of this discourse reflects where the power lies and the basis for some forms of resistance. A sense of powerlessness develops from a removal of authenticity. For students who understand this experience, they can change it:

If a person has the same power as a teacher, they can stand up to the teacher, then the teacher backs down, like [someone's] Mum. [female]

The curriculum is contested in other ways. Part of the Aboriginal Studies policy is the inclusion of Aboriginal people in the teaching. In this school, the Aboriginal Education Assistant (AEA) was doing a difficult job with the materials available. The emphasis on self-esteem through the reinforcement of a particular identity created anger among the students.

We were going to [suburb] for this performance thing. They were having a big festival. She [the AEA] stuffed the [traditional Aboriginal] food down our throats, and like we didn't want to eat it. She was stuffing the food down. And she said "You should be proud of the Abbos." I mean I am proud, but I don't want anyone else hearing about it. [female]

Unlike their parents, young Koories[4] are part of a culture influenced increasingly by global telecommunications and mass media culture. This is reflected in the pursuit of the popular African-American style, emulating male sports heroes and wearing expensive sports wear. This connection with the high fashion status of black culture may also provide the Aboriginal adolescent with vicarious status. However, the fashion trends of the young and the political sensitivity of the older generation can clash and create tension when self-conscious representations of Aboriginality such as wearing red, black, and yellow are resisted. The need to be "cool" – that is, understated trendiness in dress – is essential to youth culture.

[I feel] real ashamed when we go somewhere with her she wears all these beads right down, she wears the colored jumper [Aboriginal colors]. Yeah, everyone else turns up in their baggy jumpers and their pants [i.e., height of fashion].

Thus there is an "avowing of one's history and transforming it" (Griffiths, 1993, p. 311) within the constraints of their social conditions. Not only are there generational differences to negotiate but gendered dimensions as well. Indeed, you may have noticed in the above voices of students that the male and female positions are distinct in their sense of agency or lack of agency. Perhaps we can explore this a little more by focusing on their experiences of racism and sexism in their local area.

The older female participants experience sexism from both Anglo and Aboriginal boys who stereotype them as "sluts." Racial abuse with sexist overtones is not uncommon in their experience.

If you get pregnant it's your own fault. And also no one wants to know you. They think you're a slut.

This girl called us a black slut and I didn't want to hit her because I would have got suspended.

Even though the intersection of race and gender for females is much more pronounced than for males, girls are able to articulate more effectively their concerns about drugs and alcohol. Females also tend to be higher achievers than males in studying at the post-secondary level (Brady, 1992). The key survival strategy is reliance on the family networks, where women in particular provide the stability of the family frameworks. Throughout, the girls seemed more able to articulate the problem and a possible course of action.

Students report the latest bashings and stabbings within the local community or street gang culture and the excessive drinking on pension days:

Last week he got stabbed three times. Twice, one there and one there, and slashed him across there, and cut his face. He is in hospital. He had punctured lungs.

The school is surrounded by high wire fences to discourage vandals. Boredom and lack of leisure facilities are reported by the students and are endemic to the area. "Youths roam the streets in gangs congregating at a youth centre where a basketball court offers one of the few distractions" (Dasey, 1996). Within this disadvantaged environment, boys are expected to be tough. In another, similar context Connell (1995) notes that "through interaction in this [type of] milieu, the growing boy puts together a tense, freaky facade, making a claim to power where there are no real resources for power" (p. 111).

> *I would love one of them [fully automatic weapon] [very young male]*
>
> *If you're square, how can you fight? If you are not in a gang and you are by yourself [reference to protection in numbers].*
>
> *I love violence…I got told that there was this written on the wall, that Aboriginals could kill FOBS [fresh off the boat, slang for Islanders] and FOBS could kill Aboriginals. [young male]*

In the context of poverty, argues Connell, the dominant or hegemonic masculinity of any society is reworked into a "protest masculinity" (1995, p. 114). The male adolescents in this study have much to against which to protest.

> *[The suburb where we live] is really violent. But that's what area you're in really, like if you're over near the pub and when they come home from the pub they are really drunk and smashing bottles and things like that.*
>
> *I want to go [to another suburb]. There's always fights next door to our house.*
>
> *They have bombs next door. Yeah, they're fire bombs, petrol bombs.*
>
> *My brother won't go to sleep by himself in the room. He waits for X to go to sleep and then he goes to sleep.*
>
> *Our next door neighbor always bashes the kids, they're only two or three. She has been arrested about seven times, but she still does it.*

The social space in which cultures are shaped creates tensions that require an approach to self-esteem that does more than operate on the individual.

Conclusion

If we accept that culture is dynamic and continually constituted then the self is continually constituted. Griffiths (1993) argues that we ought to link self-esteem with theories of subjectivity rather than the self. In this way there is recognition of political groupings. That is, the importance of how peoples see themselves in relation to others and how they are shaped in interaction with others (inter-subjectivity). "The evidence is, that an understanding of racism and sexism helps self-esteem and can also help change patterns of achievement" (Griffiths, 1993, p. 314). Alternative curricula have been devised, in particular, a series called Social Literacy (Cope and Kalantzis, 1990).

Perhaps the final word from Aboriginal academic Pat Dudgeon (1990) and non-Aboriginal educators Simone Lazaroo and Harry Picket sums up the self-esteem approach best.

Myths and strategies to make people feel happier and more passively accepting of their lot are common in the history of caste and class systems.

For Aboriginal girls, as for Aboriginal people, self-esteem programs ask the wrong questions and offer wrong answers. Community self-determination and individual self-determination are indivisible for Aboriginal people. Without them, self-esteem programs are irrelevant and contrived. If Aboriginal education is "self-determined", self-esteem programs are unnecessary.

Notes

[1] During an interview, one female student quoted her grandmother as referring to the children of black and white parents as "magpie babies." Magpies are black and white birds indigenous to Australia. The term was also used in a television drama called Heartlands, an Australia Broadcasting Commission production about a relationship between an Aboriginal man and a white woman.

[2] See *Bringing Them Home*, a guide to the findings and recommendations of the national inquiry into the separation of Aboriginal and Torres Strait Islander children from their families.

[3] Australia is one of the most highly urbanized countries in the world. The level of urbanization is around 85%. Over 80% of people are along the eastern and southeastern coastal regions. In land terms this is 3.3% of national land area. Forty percent of the total population lives in Melbourne or Sydney. Castles et al. (1997), *Australia and Immigration: A Partnership*, p. 37.

[4] Koori: meaning Aboriginal person from the south-east of Australia. Includes Victoria, Tasmania and half of New South Wales. Used here since it is how the students named themselves.

References

Brady, M. 1992. *The Health of Young Aborigines: A Report on the Health of Aborigines Aged 12 to 25 Years*. Tasmania: National Clearing House for Youth Studies.

Collins, J. 1991. *Migrant Hands in a Distant Land*. Sydney: Pluto Press.

Connell, R. W. 1987. *Gender and Power*. London: Polity Press

Connell, R. W. 1995. "Live Fast and Die Young." In *Masculinities*, pp. 89-119. Berkeley: University of California Press.

Cope, B., Kalantzis, M. 1990. "Cultural Differences and Self-Esteem: Alternative Curriculum Approaches." In *Hearts and Minds: Self-Esteem and the Schooling of Girls*, edited by Jane Kenway and Sue Willis, pp. 159-72. London: Falmer.

Daniels, Douglas. 1986."The Coming Crisis in the Indigenous Rights Movement: From Colonialism to Neo-Colonialism to Renaissance." In *Native Studies Review*, vol. 2, no. 2:97-115.

Dasey, Daniel. 1996. "Bored and Lodging." *The Sun-Herald*, 4 February.

Dudgeon, P.; Lazaroo, S.; Pickett, H. 1990. "Aboriginal Girls: Self-Esteem or Self-Determination?" In *Hearts and Minds: Self-Esteem and the Schooling of Girls*, edited by Jane Kenway and Sue Willis, pp. 71-96. London: Falmer.

Fay, Brian. 1996. "Do You Have to be One to Know One?" In *Contemporary Philosophy of Social Science*, pp. 9-29. Oxford: Blackwell.

Fletcher, J. J. 1989a. *Clean, Clad and Courteous: A History of Aboriginal Education in New South Wales*. Carlton: J. Fletcher.

Fletcher, J. J. 1989b. *Documents in the History of Aboriginal Education in New South Wales*. Carlton: J. Fletcher.

Goodall, Heather. 1996. *Invasion to Embassy: Land in Aboriginal Politics in New South Wales, 1770-1972*. Sydney: Allen and Unwin.

Grace, H.; Hage, G.; Johnson, L.; Langsworth, J. and Symonds, M. 1997. *Home World - Space, Community and Marginality in Sydney's West*. Sydney: Pluto.

Griffiths, Morwenna. 1993. "Self-Identity and Self-Esteem: Achieving Equality in Education." *Oxford Review of Education 19*, no. 3: 301-17.

Hall, Stuart. 1996. "Introduction: Who Needs Identity?" In *Questions of Cultural Identity*, edited by Stuart Hall and Paul Du Gay, pp. 1-17. Sage: London.

House of Representatives Standing Committee on Aboriginal and Torres Strait Islander Affairs. (1992). *Mainly Urban*. Report of the Inquiry into the Needs of Urban Dwelling Aboriginal and Torres Strait Islander People. Canberra: Australian Government Publishing.

Kalantzis, Mary; Cope, Bill; Noble, Greg; Poynting, Scott. 1990. "A Systems Perspective." In *Cultures of Schooling: Pedagogies for Cultural Difference and Social Access*, pp. 15-39. Hampshire: Falmer Press.

Keeffe, Kevin. 1992. *From the Centre to the City: Aboriginal Education, Culture and Power*. Canberra: Aboriginal Studies Press.

Langton, Marcia. 1981. "Urbanizing Aborigines: The Social Scientists' Great Deception." *Social Alternatives 2*, no. 2:

Lipka, Jerry. 1990. "Cross-Cultural Perceptions of Teaching Styles." *Kaurna Higher Education Journal*, no. 1 (September): 33-42.

Malin, Merridy. 1990. "Invisibility and Visibility of the Aboriginal Child in an Urban Classroom." *Australian Journal of Education 34*, no. 3: 312-39.

Millis, Roger. 1994. *Waterloo Creek: The Australia Day Massacre of 1838, George Gipps and the British Conquest of New South Wales*. Sydney: University of NSW Press.

National Review of Education for Aboriginal and Torres Strait Islander Peoples - Final Report. 1995. Canberra: Department of Employment, Education and Training.

Nicholls, Christine; Crowley, Vicki; and Watt, Ron. 1996. "Theorising Aboriginal Education: Surely It's Time to Move On?" *Education Australia*, no. 33: 6-9.

Troyna, Barry. 1992. "Multicultural and Anti-Racist Education Policies." In *Racism and Education: Structures and Strategies*, edited by D. Gill, B. Mayor, and M. Blair. London: Sage.

Wammarra Aboriginal Education Centre. 1992. The First of Its Kind: NSW Aboriginal Education Policy Implementation Evaluation, volume 1, Report. Sydney: NSW Department of School Education.

Chapter 2
Changing Perspectives on Intercultural Classrooms

Angela Ward, University of Saskatchewan, Canada

Coalition-building across cultures is a particularly delicate task, given the "researched" history of Aboriginal peoples. In this chapter I reach a tentative rapprochement with my own guilt as I describe my experiences of collaborative research in urban settings. In my understanding of social justice issues for Aboriginal children in Canadian schools, I have followed a path sign-posted by researchers from different educational traditions. In education, as in the natural sciences, we tend to espouse the notion that progress always entails leaving behind previous ideas, sometimes forgetting hard-won wisdom. In this chapter I will retrace some of my own steps in order to arrive at new insights about classroom research in intercultural settings.

I began my research career looking at the daily interactions between teachers and their students, expecting that Aboriginal underachievement in North American schools could be attributed to differential discourse patterns. From there I have moved to a recognition that the experiences of Aboriginal students in our schools are part of the colonial imperialism imposed by European invaders. But as a teacher educator, I also need to balance the broad sweep of postcolonial theory with the responsibility to create communities of care in our schools. I have returned to the belief that it is important to direct our thoughtful gaze on the minutiae of classroom life. Our ability to fully see and understand the effects of oppression on the detail of students' classroom lives makes us critically conscious teachers.

My passionate concern for the relations between Aboriginal and non-Aboriginal peoples in Canada had a pragmatic origin. Since my family and I were in a small community where Aboriginal and non-Aboriginal people lived in close proximity, I needed to understand the racism and anger I saw rise to the surface of daily encounters between people in my town. After I became a teacher, my questions became more urgent, as I struggled to make my classroom a safe and respectful place where all students could meet my expectations for academic success. I went to graduate school looking for the answers to my Aboriginal students' difficulties in reading, the resistance of older students to the traditions of mainstream school structures, and the intolerance demonstrated by non-Aboriginal teenagers towards their Aboriginal peers. This chapter describes the varied understandings I gained along a somewhat convoluted research journey, and suggests that socio-linguistic and ethnographic perspectives still have a place in the political landscape of current intercultural research in school settings. The concept of communicative inequality is useful in describing how Aboriginal students have been silenced by the micro-events of mainstream classrooms, the participant structures of schooling and societal relations with European colonizers.

The study I carried out in the 1980s (Ward, 1990) focused on the communicative inequality experienced by Aboriginal students in the kindergarten classroom where I was for a year a participant observer. I was led to the study because of my excitement that language variability rather than deficit might be an "explanation" of the school difficulties encountered by my Aboriginal students. At that time, compensatory language programs based on the Headstart model had been used in an effort to improve the academic performance of Aboriginal students. Language difficulties had been frequently cited as a major cause for the educational problems of Aboriginal students.

As the problems of minority groups were considered in the context of broader views of language development, educational researchers turned to the study of classroom language use, employing naturalistic methodology (Mehan, 1979). Such studies indicated that difference in language function might be an important clue to the poor academic performance of some individuals and groups. Other studies (Erickson and Mohatt, 1982; Philips, 1983) strongly suggested that differences in participant and communicative structures might be restricting the chances of Aboriginal students for school success. I believed that since the school domain was one where Aboriginal students were most likely to experience communicative inequality, it was a useful context in which to collect evidence for the cultural variability of the language spoken by Aboriginal students. The purpose of my dissertation study was to document the beginning school experience of a cross-cultural kindergarten class through detailed participant observation. In describing children's construction and understanding of the socio-linguistic rules of their classroom, I hoped to contribute knowledge to the fight for social justice, at least in schools.

The study clearly documented the communicative inequality experienced by Aboriginal students in a Canadian public school. I noted that, if cultural variability in language use is one valid explanation of school failure, then an understanding of its origins and maintenance will be useful to teachers working with Aboriginal students (Ward, 1990). During the course of this study, I spent over 50 days in the kindergarten classroom audio-taping nine Aboriginal and five non-Aboriginal children and their teacher in daily whole-group discussions. I conducted a time-consuming analysis of the resulting transcripts, looking at participation and question and response patterns. Additionally, I placed this analysis within the community experiences and broad language domains of Mountainview.

What was it, then, about the language of schools that caused the Aboriginal students in this study so much difficulty? The reasons for the low participation of students in instructional dialogue were found in the interactional structures of classroom life. Cook-Gumperz (1986) separated the acquisition of literacy and the process of schooling, regarding the latter as a force in the selective transmission of knowledge. This "schooled literacy" became associated with a set of controlling behaviors, acculturating the child to a hierarchical society. Within the microcosm of the classroom, this hierarchy is recreated with the teacher as its head. In my study, as in others, it was the teacher who talked most of the time, and determined who else was able to talk, and for how long. The form of dialogue used by teachers for instruction and discussion is highly predictable across classrooms in North America and Britain, and its existence in my study reduced the classroom participation of all children, but especially those from Aboriginal backgrounds.

The almost invariable instructional routine of elicitation (usually in the form of a question), student response, and teacher feedback has been described extensively in the literature (Mehan, 1979; Sinclair and Coulthard, 1975). Brice Heath (1982) suggested that the problems of African American children in mainstream schools were at least partially attributable to the fact that "school questions were unfamiliar in their frequency, purposes and types, and in the domains of content knowledge and skills display they assumed on the part of students" (p. 123). Philips (1983) stated that the difference between school and home verbal interaction strategies was a major barrier to Aboriginal success in the North American public school system.

The static nature of children's contributions to instructional dialogue illustrated the power of form over function. Traditional patterns of teacher-student interaction appeared to inhibit the children's development of heuristic and imaginative language functions in this setting. The form of instructional dialogue logically limited the length and frequency of all students' contributions, but particularly inhibited the participation of Aboriginal students. This power imbalance between participants in an instructional event was also noted by Au (1980) in a study of Hawaiian children's participation in small group reading lessons. The redress of the "balance of rights" became the focus for changing teacher behavior in later studies. In my study, the power imbalance was a major contributor in the low participation of children in instructional dialogue.

There were clear reasons why Aboriginal students did not follow the rules of instructional dialogue as readily as non-Aboriginal children. In general the Aboriginal children did not understand the dialogue rules, and spoke for other children more frequently than their non-Aboriginal peers. They were also more confused by the multiplicity of rules attendant on different types of dialogue. This resulted in awkwardness when the teacher tried to correct an "unoriginal" response in show and tell, or when students commented on personal concerns at inappropriate times. It also led the children to amazing ingenuity in circumventing rules. During one discussion, the students were asked to give examples of food eaten by bears. Kyle had responded "Fish," but in applying the rule that all answers must be original, the teacher had rejected Don's "Fish" answer as unacceptable. He thought for a while, and then answered loudly "Two fish," indicating at once his understanding and disdain for the rule. Aboriginal children experienced discomfort when asked to respond in ways that conflicted with their early socialization. This discomfort was shown in the high proportion of non-responses, extremely low voice volume and short (often one-word) answers. Girls were more likely to manifest this than boys. As a result of this study I came to understand the importance of classroom participant structures in supporting inclusion of all students' voices. Dialogue structures that were literally foreign to half their participants alienated the very children whose language they were supposed to develop.

When I moved to Saskatchewan after completing this study, I became interested in the intercultural communication between urban Aboriginal students and their classmates and teachers. I had much to learn about the challenges facing Aboriginal students in urban settings, but discovered that communicative inequality was manifested in similar ways in intercultural classrooms in my new home. My first study had not involved the teacher except as a person to be watched and commented upon. When I reflected back on this work, I felt shame that I had not supported the classroom teacher in changing interaction patterns to benefit her students. My resolution was to engage the teacher and students in my next project in order to build better intercultural communication. I worked with an experienced teacher in a collaborative study whose aim was to teach beginning primary children to work together. We planned co-operative partner activities and small group talk activities, and jointly implemented them over several years. The students in her classroom were fairly typical of the mix of students in Saskatchewan's small cities. About 80 percent of the students were from diverse Aboriginal backgrounds, including Cree, Dene, Lakota and Métis. The other students were from eastern European and northern European backgrounds, with one or two children from immigrant Asian families. The children from Aboriginal backgrounds had varying degrees of exposure to traditional Aboriginal cultures. Several were being raised in the city by grandparents who still spoke Cree or Dene, while others had significant contact with extended families on a northern reserve where they visited at holiday times and through the summer. Still others lived in the city with urbanized parents, who for a number of reasons had very little contact with their Aboriginal roots. However, there were similarities between these urban Aboriginal children and those I had loved in my small British Columbia community. The Aboriginal girls in this class were much quieter than the boys, even in small group interactions. In large group talk, the non-Aboriginal students still tended to dominate interactions with the teacher and with me.

I also noticed differences between the urban community surrounding the school and the small Aboriginal village where I had previously taught. When children were in trouble in the rural community, I could phone an aunt or ask a cousin to take a child home. In the city, help could be found, but it was most likely from an official source (Social Services or the police). The bureaucratization of support services seems to be an inevitable result of living in communities where members did not know or trust each other. There was an Aboriginal network of families in the neighborhood, but they were not always in daily contact as they might have been in a small community. Children did not have the same sense of connection with each other that they had in Mountainview, British Columbia. In the rural community this connection was shown through shared narratives of experience, where children talked about their joint excursions to pick "sunflowers" (balsam) or to watch a family friend skinning a bear. In the urban environment children lived more physically confined lives. Few of them met each other outside school, so their shared conversations tended to focus on T.V. and video shows.

During my time in this urban classroom, I was searching for the type of participant structure that would engage children most deeply in thoughtful conversations with each other. The teacher and I, two European women, explicitly "modelled" ways of talking to each other that included social and interactional conventions: we asked each other politely for scissors, made suggestions for story ideas, or helped each other remember the names of characters in a favorite story. We had long debates about whether we were demonstrating Eurocentric dialogue conventions that were inappropriate for our students, but decided that we needed to highlight the role of language in co-operative activity. Some students participated without difficulty in small group work, but for most children partner interaction most readily supported intercultural conversations. Despite our success in encouraging co-operative work, Aboriginal girls still had difficulty in breaking into conversations with boys. Our solution was to put Aboriginal girls together, which was probably culturally appropriate at some levels, but did nothing to change the behavior of boys who did not allow space for others.

It became clear to me that appropriate participant structures were only one aspect of a culturally responsive environment for Aboriginal students as I spent time in Maureen's classroom. [Her class is described in more detail in Ward, 1996.] Maureen brought her Cree background to teaching in a number of ways. Most obviously, there were pictures and resource materials reflecting Aboriginal experiences everywhere in her room. She produced her own posters and pictures, and found everything with an Aboriginal focus that she could order from the school board's resource centre. One important result of this was that students clustered around pictures of Aboriginal people and northern animals, and conversed seriously about experiences of their own evoked by the wall displays.

Maureen's own gentleness and indirect style of disciplining students contributed to a deep comfort within the classroom, for students and visitors alike. I grew to look forward to the part of my week I would spend in her room, because, in synchrony with the rhythms of her interactions with the students, I became less harried and more in tune with what children had to say. I believe that this relaxed informality with children had its roots in Maureen's deep understanding of herself-in-relation with the students. More than once, she referred to them as her family, and invited her own family members to be part of her class. Maureen's father was a particularly favorite visitor. Watching his loving care of her and of her students brought to mind Graveline's reminder that "Community is a sacred concept with high value in Aboriginal culture" (1998, p. 164).

Maureen had great success with mainstream co-operative learning techniques, as well as with a version of the Cree talking circle. She used the talking circle structure to replace "show and tell." It was a stunning contrast to the discussions I had watched in Mountainview. A rock was passed hand to hand around the circle, and children chose whether or not to make a spoken contribution. On several occasions, the group of 22 Grade 1 students would sit quietly for 90 seconds waiting for a child to say something, and when nothing was forthcoming the rock simply passed on and no comments were made. Early in the year, many students passed up the opportunity to participate, but by October, almost all students took a turn. This was in contrast to the Mountainview group, where Aboriginal students participated less and less frequently as the year progressed (Ward, 1989).

My role as researcher was to explain what was happening in Maureen's classroom. Certainly my discourse analysis made it clear that participation in classroom discussions was increased through the strategies Maureen used, but, of course, the rich life of the classroom, and the story of Maureen-in-relation is not told through an account of one participant structure. Her classroom came close to the ideal of communicative equality, and I could certainly identify some reasons for this. At this point in my academic career I felt it was insufficient to describe and analyze teaching in intercultural settings. As one of the liberals despised by critical educators, I moved from the intimacy of single classroom studies to join a network of educators interested in intercultural teaching and learning. In my next life I will come back as a revolutionary fighting for social justice, but I am constrained in this life by my upbringing as a conventional, fairly timid, white woman. This network of Aboriginal and non-Aboriginal academics and school researchers has undertaken a number of collaborative studies (for example, Legare et al., 1999; Ward and Wason-Ellam, 1995). The various projects have had slightly different aims, but their overall intent has been to support teachers in intercultural educational settings, and to engage with them in conversations about their experiences. This work brings diverse women together in the quest for practical wisdom and seeks to mitigate, albeit on a very small stage, effects of colonization on the relationship between Aboriginal and non-Aboriginal peoples in the Canadian school system. The network has used similar methodologies, mixed in different proportions, for each study. There has usually been a combination of face-to-face network meetings, individual interviews, fieldwork and active participation in classrooms by the academics in the network.

In her broad discussion of interpretive reviews, Eisenhart (1998) asks a number of questions pertinent to research in intercultural settings. Strong interpretive research should "reveal alternative ways of making sense of educational phenomena" and "startle readers out of mainstream complacency about educational issues" (p. 397). There have been moments where at least my own beliefs have been disrupted by what I have found in a research project, but I still hold to the importance of relationship in teaching and research. The centrality of the teacher-student-community relationship in the educational process has been reaffirmed by recent explorations of school-community connections in an urban setting (Wason-Ellam and Ward, 1998). As part of this study I interviewed five teachers about their own literacy beliefs and experiences. These five women, who at a superficial glance would appear to have had very different early lives (two were Aboriginal and one had moved to Canada from Europe), in fact had common experiences with literacy at home and at school. Their own literacy backgrounds were quite similar to those of the children whom they taught. What differentiated these teachers was how early encounters with books had affected their classroom practice. The professional training they had all received in colleges of education tended to provide the non-Aboriginal teachers with a cognitive view of their role as literacy educators, while the Aboriginal teachers envisioned literacy as a tool through which values and respect for others might be learned. Yet all the teachers in this study recalled their pleasure in reading with family members, and their distress when classmates were humiliated by reading difficulties. It was the Aboriginal teachers who maintained their consistency as teachers-in-relation in academic areas.

Thus in my ten years as a researcher, I have come to realize that there are many pathways which could lead to social justice in language arts classrooms. Recognition of the political realities of colonization for Aboriginal people today enables us to see how the power imbalances of North American society are still reflected in classrooms through communicative inequality. Is it possible that educational research has a role in creating classrooms which are more respectful of urban Aboriginal children's needs? I believe that cross-cultural participatory research that involves Aboriginal researchers and teachers does have the potential to create change at the micro level of the classroom and perhaps at the system level.

When I began educational research a decade ago, I was still looking for answers to specific educational questions. Now I am hoping to enrich my understanding of life in classrooms, but, beyond that, to influence changes in educational practice so that social justice might flourish in classroom communities. For more than that, I will have to wait until my next life.

References

Au, K. H. 1980. "Participation Structures in a Reading Lesson with Hawaiian Children: Analysis of a Culturally Appropriate Instructional Event." *Anthropology and Education Quarterly 11*: 91-115.

Brice-Heath, S. 1983. *Ways with Words.* Cambridge: Cambridge University Press.

Cook-Gumperz, J., ed. 1986. *The Social Construction of Literacy.* Cambridge: Cambridge University Press.

Dumont, R. V. 1972. "Learning English and How to be Silent: Studies in Sioux and Cherokee Classrooms." In *Functions of Language in the Classroom*, edited by C. Cazden, V. John, and D. Hymes. New York: Teachers College Press.

Eisenhart, M. 1998. "On the Subject of Interpretive Reviews." *Review of Educational Research 68*, no. 4 (winter): 391-99.

Erickson, F., and Mohatt, G. 1982. "Cultural Organization of Participation Structures in Two Classrooms of Indian Students." In *Doing the Ethnography of Schooling*, edited by G. Spindler. New York: Holt, Rinehart and Winston.

Graveline, F. G. 1998. *Circle Works: Transforming Eurocentric Consciousness.* Halifax: Fernwood Publishing.

Legare, L.; Pete-Willett, S.; Ward, A.; Wason-Ellam, L.; Williamson, K. 1998. *Diverting the Mainstream: Aboriginal Teachers Reflect on Their Experiences in Saskatchewan Provincial Schools.* Regina, SK: Saskatchewan Education.

Mehan, H. 1979. *Learning Lessons: Social Organization in the Classroom.* Cambridge, MA: Harvard University Press.

Philips, S. U. 1983. *The Invisible Culture.* New York: Longman.

Sinclair, J. M., and Coulthard, R. M. 1975. *Towards an Analysis of Discourse: The English Used by Teachers and Pupils.* London: Oxford University Press.

Ward, A. 1997. *Classroom Conversations: Talking and Learning in Elementary Schools.* Toronto: Nelson.

Ward, A. 1996. "Beyond 'Sharing Time': Negotiating Aboriginal Culture in an Urban Classroom." *English Quarterly 28*, nos. 2 and 3: 23-28.

Ward, A. 1990. "Communicative Inequality: The Participation of Native Indian and Non-Native Children in Instructional Dialogue in a Cross-Cultural Kindergarten Class." *Reading-Canada-Lecture 8*, no. 1: 22-29.

Ward, A. 1989. "Communicative Inequality: The Participation of Native Indian and Non-Native Children in Instructional Dialogue in a Cross-Cultural Kindergarten Class." Ph.D. dissertation, University of Victoria.

Ward, A.; Wason-Ellam, L.; and an inner-city teacher team. 1995. *Supporting Literacy Instruction in Cross-Cultural Classrooms.* Saskatoon, SK: Dr. Stirling McDowell Foundation for Research into Teaching, Inc.

Wason-Ellam, L.; Ward, A.; and Williamson, K. 1998. *Giving Voice to Teachers: Finding Common Ground through Action Research.* Saskatoon, SK: Dr. Stirling McDowell Foundation for Research into Teaching, Inc.

Section Two

Surviving the City: Stories of Identities Lost and Regained

Chapter 3

Good Community Schools Are Sites of Educational Activism

Rita Bouvier, Metis,
Saskatchewan Teachers Federation, Canada

This chapter explores a vision for community schools/education as a journey toward the discovery of ourselves, at a local and global level. Applying a theoretical definition of community schools, the vision seeks to balance short and long term purposes of education; it seeks to establish trust and respect in relationships; it places value on the gifts that everyone brings to this endeavor; and finally, it seeks results that honor all life. The ideas explored are based on selected literature, community school evaluations in Saskatchewan and the inspiration of dreams that promise hope for our children.

This is a revision of a paper developed for an annual conference of the Community Schools Association of Saskatchewan. The organizers of the conference invited a critical and renewed look at community schools. The theoretical definition applied in this exploration warranted that I place myself as a participant, given the responsibility I have in the community. To challenge our current conception of community schools I asked questions rhetorically, at times. I reflected upon and celebrated the accomplishments of the program. Since then, community schools in Saskatchewan have had a renewed mandate as expressed in a policy statement titled, interestingly enough, *Building Communities of Hope* (Saskatchewan Education, 1996). It has extended the designation of community schools to northern schools.

The historical context and development of community schools in North America, and specifically the province of Saskatchewan, are perhaps best exemplified by a quotation that comes from the initial evaluation done on community schools approximately a decade ago.

> *The community schools program is without a doubt, the largest and most successful program directed toward the social problems of inner city students in any Canadian province. It bridges the gap between the culture of the school and the culture of the home. (Saskatchewan Education, 1984)*

It is a program directed toward a specific population, which is not made explicit in this earlier text. The issues confronting us in this context are viewed and analyzed as "social" problems. In addition, bridging what is viewed as a cultural gap between the school and the home is viewed as a central issue. It suggests we have strong emotional ties to these programs. That was ten years ago; has our thinking changed?

Since then, much has changed at both provincial and federal levels. Controlling deficits, restructuring and globalization are the buzz words of political agendas at both levels. In Saskatchewan, we have developed a new model for delivery of services to "at risk" families and children, the integrated school linked services model. It invites all the agencies involved with the lives of families and children "at risk" to work together. It makes good sense, but it also holds some challenges, the most critical one being the need for a clear understanding of roles, relationships and responsibilities of the agencies involved and the beneficiaries themselves. What will be their role, relationship and responsibility to the vision articulated? From a service delivery viewpoint, there are ethical considerations about the information shared.

The questions I have raised are explored through a framework of community schools offered by Sharilyn Calliou, a Cree-Mohawk woman. Sharilyn Calliou (1993) offers the community school model as way of promoting and supporting "healthy" sovereignty for First Nation communities for both rural and urban environments. The work is based on 30 articles theorizing on the idea of community schools. She writes, "In community schools theory, community is identified as a laboratory for community-based teaching, learning and planned change." Education in this context is people-centred, problem-centred and community-centred. Summarizing the definition of community, based on a cross-cultural exploration, she identifies four components: first, there must be participants and that our definition of participants must move beyond a human one, to one that is inclusive of all species; second, there is a need to comprehend thoroughly the nature and inventory of the elements and relationships evident within a locale; third, there is a need to understand the common premise for choosing to live in a certain way; and finally, certain results are expected, if we are to be successful in lasting change and if we are to achieve social justice.

A re-examination of the idea of community schools/education is a timely one, given the quest and emphasis for community in the literature. Perhaps, it promises to fill the spiritual void that many of us feel. For example, Sergiovanni (1993, 1994), a leading theorist on educational leadership and administration, offers community as a future metaphor for the organization of schools; and promotes schools as "community learning centres." As an aside, I offer an observation I have made on the recent literature, particularly surrounding leadership: a congruence between Indigenous thought and philosophy is growing. This recognition is important to Indigenous peoples around the world as they seek changes for their communities and define a new relationship with peoples in their respective homelands (World Conference of Indigenous Peoples on Education, 1993). As Indigenous people, the richness we can provide to the human family is not material. I had almost forgotten. In a school visit in the northern region of New Zealand, during my sabbatical, I met a little young person I will not forget. After sharing a few comments about myself and the land I had come from, she insisted on getting my attention with a question that I decided, at the time, was out of place. She asked me the same question three times before I answered her. The question was, "Are you rich?" On the third count, my mouth opened and the words were to this effect: "Yes, oh, yes I am very rich." I went on to list the names of my extended family, my friends, my son, to which she responded, "Like you, I am very rich."

Comprehending Thoroughly the Nature of the Elements and the Relationships of a Locale

Let me return, then, to the historical and present context of community schools as they exist in Saskatchewan. If there is no attempt to understand the nature of the elements and relationships of the locale, there can be little meaning to our discussion and the future. The first recognizable fact of the inner city is one of poverty. In Saskatchewan, and I suspect elsewhere, there is a complex dimension to the nature of this poverty because it arises out of situations of chronic unemployment, poor education, illness and deep-seated systemic issues. Large segments of the population served by community schools in Saskatchewan are Aboriginal people. Poverty involves economic deprivation with its own brand of social and psychological impact, regardless of who the people are in a cultural sense. Segments of the population living in the inner city are easily identifiable because of the color of their skin and perhaps because of their gender. Therefore, it is about power, which is often dictated by people in a more privileged position. There is a tendency to label and therefore misrepresent the diverse group of people who live within this locality.

Connell (1994), a professor of studies in sociology of education, observes that educational systems generally have been less than successful with many programs directed toward the poor. The deficit and compensatory nature of many programs do little other than to reinforce the stereotypes held of the population. The issues facing members of this community are economic, political, cultural and yes, social. The inequities that face people living in these environments are systemic – meaning they are ingrained structurally within society and therefore the issues that confront people in the inner cities belong to all of us. The statistics and demography in this province suggest that poverty is casting a wider net. To rectify the political, economic, cultural and social issues faced by people with little, if any, income requires us to examine not so much what is happening locally but what is happening globally. Connell observes that those likely to understand the issues – namely, the poor, and the teachers who work most directly with the children in the schools – are often objects of policy and decisions rather than authors of it. To rethink what we do, Connell suggests that we begin with an examination of power that is evident in the politics of mass education, a hegemonic mainstream curriculum and the character of teachers' work. Secondly, he suggests that we accept the economics of poverty. Poverty is poverty; it implies a scarcity of resources. If we are to achieve social justice, it implies a higher level of funding for schools that serve communities that are poor. Until 1996, there had been no additional funding to community schools in Saskatchewan since 1982. According to one source, funds were frozen from 1983 to 1989. The increase of 3 percent in 1990 reflected money provided for special projects (Smadu, 1991). In educational terms, Connell (1994) argues for a shift in pedagogy and the way content is determined. Freire (1999) reinforces the importance of teachers respecting not only the knowledge of the popular classes, but also knowledge from communities that are often neglected by authorities.

The next consideration for understanding the locale of community schools is the infrastructure within which they currently operate. They exist within the context of a board of education that often serves a larger community, and, of course, the board itself operates within a provincial legislative and policy framework. It is perhaps the rigidity of this system that frustrates the work of those involved most directly and actively (Saskatchewan Education, 1984; Smadu, 1991). Achieving social justice through education is not a neutral undertaking. Those who are committed to this goal come to understand that it usually requires flexibility within all the systems operating, whether they are boards of education, or provincial or national bodies. Addressing the social and psychological effects of poverty is not easy. Children do not learn when they are hungry, abused or angry. These are issues that cannot be ignored. Ask the teachers and the parents. Schools and teachers, alone, cannot address these issues, and technical educational solutions are not sufficient.

An earlier observation was made that large segments of the inner city population are Aboriginal people. The impact of colonization on Aboriginal people must be understood and confronted if we are to be successful in supporting the students in their education. It requires examination of the past and present conditions. History and context are critical elements for understanding the issues facing us. As Hampton (1993) has argued, we need a sense of history that does not avoid the hard facts. Unfortunately, we cannot say that we have entirely escaped the colonial relationship of the past. As teachers, we must balance this discussion by giving equal emphasis to an examination of a new relationship; to model it; to live it as we interact with each other and our students. Otherwise, the goals of equity and social justice are empty rhetoric. It is uncomfortable work, but necessary, if we are to confront the helplessness felt at an individual, and sometimes a collective, level. As Mary Marule, a community educator said at a MOKAKIT conference I attended in Calgary, Alberta, in 1995, "Aboriginal people need to develop political consciousness." When we attend to the education of Aboriginal children we cannot be unengaged politically; we must have a clear bias. Their education must be affirming physically, of who they are as a people, it must be intellectually engaging, spiritually embracing and emotionally supportive (Mello et al., 1994). The work of educators in community schools involves the real lives of children who are oppressed, poor and often disenfranchised. Those who work centrally within the larger infrastructure of the educational system have a duty to support and encourage the people who serve these communities, and to advocate for them.

Governments have an equally critical role to play. Their economic and social policy must work hand in hand with educational policy if the goals for social justice and equity are to be achieved. The emphasis on deficits, the erosion of universal social programs and the ideology of "choice" where education is concerned puts people experiencing poverty most at risk and ultimately does so to everyone else as well (Barlow and Robertson, 1994).

In this examination of the elements and relationships of the community school's locale, I have attempted to broaden the sphere, influence and impact. The temptation is to view locales narrowly. I have attempted to broaden this idea of community into a larger sphere focusing at the central point of planning and decision making in the education system and elsewhere, such as government. Perhaps I should have included "big business," since it has a major influence on the political agenda and therefore on public policy. What are the assumptions of the restructuring directed to so-called families and students at risk? I hope "Brighter Futures" and "Children First" are more than catchy policy titles and slogans. Will the programs prematurely stream so-called "children at risk" to jobs at the bottom end? What is the underlying economic policy? Does it view children as more than a supply of labor?

Despite my scepticism of provincial and federal policy, I am fully aware that when it comes to breathing life into these "targeted" programs, the unsung people at the front lines will make the difference as they have always done. From my vantage point, transcending the shortcomings of these types of programs has become an art, in and of itself. When there is no choice but to accept the terms and conditions of scarce money, individuals can turn the fish and loaves to feed six, to feed thousands. We do not celebrate these individuals often enough.

Critical policy decisions are often made far and away from the point of impact. Therefore, it is important that when we begin to rewrite a vision of community schools we give equal attention to the complex elements of the physical locale and the central places where decisions are made. Disadvantage is an outcome of advantage. If we are really serious about the goals of equity and social justice, we will give equal attention to broader legislation and policy, ensuring that as a base it attends to people most in need of change, first. Indeed, I would suggest that the foundational premise of all public policy should begin with the people most in need, if governments are serious about the goals of equity and social justice. In isolation, add-on targeted programs are at best a band-aid solution, with a tendency to subject their recipients to stigmatization and political hostility (Connell, 1994).

Communicating and Understanding the Common Premise for Choosing to Live in a Certain Way

At a recent conference on Multicultural, Inter-cultural and Race Relations Education held in Vancouver in November 1993, I was invited along with two other Aboriginal educators to sit on a panel entitled "Focus on Empowerment Through Inclusion: First Nations People." I was asked to focus my comments on education for Aboriginal youth. I shared my own story, remembering my late grandfather's way of responding to important issues or questions. I analyzed the issues confronting youth and reflected on the strategies we employed in our communities and institutions based on hopes and dreams for my own son. I share a summary of my comments here, to begin a discussion about a common premise for education and for choosing to live in a certain way. There were two foundational premises to my proposal: first that our children are not our possessions, but extensions of our own human existence; secondly, as parents and adults, despite the different roles we fulfill in our lifetime, we are responsible for providing the pattern for behavior that respects all life. We do so by employing various strategies; ritual and ceremony are traditional practices that remind us of our relationships to each other and this physical place that we understand sustains our life – all life. Lamonthe (1994) has identified other strategies we might employ, such as: physical demonstration and observation to develop skill; giving emphasis to what we eat – behavior and diet are linked – providing occasion for sacrifice as preparation for the long journey; employing indirect strategies to show respect and to save face – anger and embarrassment lead to a closed mind – valuing mistakes as a valid premise for learning; teaching in isolation; using stories to guide development of young people, providing oral guidance and finally providing time for dreaming and fasting-reflective techniques that provide new insight and information. We also need to remember that example and nature teach.

I observed that many issues facing Aboriginal youth are symptoms of deeper needs that include identity and acceptance or belonging. I argued that tolerance, appreciation and liberal forms of inclusion were not acceptable. Aboriginal children, and for that matter all children, need nothing less than acceptance and love as a base to guide them in their learning and development. With respect to identity, I argued for forms that were not fixed but fluid and multiple. What is needed is a strong cultural identity: strong identities as men and women, a national identity and a strong human identity.

In my examination of the strategies we employed to fulfill youth needs, I observed that the most innovative and critical strategies, those having a long term effect, often placed trust in the youth to make responsible choices. In these instances, youth were given the opportunity to gain valuable knowledge, skills and ways of being – to choose a good path through guidance of a caring adult. Such programs required youth to think for themselves, to assume responsibility for their behavior, now. Institutional response, on the other hand, employed "more of the same" over an extended period or employ controlling strategies.

This led me to conclude that we were compelled to examine, to develop and to support an education that had as its core: a conserving capacity that examines values, behavior, roles and relationships based on hope and love for our children; a creative capacity that seeks changes for a better way to live engendered with responsibility and care; and last, a critical capacity that reads beyond the word to understand the basis and value of power through a person's own volition. I argued that education premised on ethnocentric views, on principles skewed toward competition, on ignorance and hate rather than on knowledge resonant with wisdom, compassion and a sense of an ethic, would not serve my son or future generations. The education I envisioned would place value on culture and language because it forms the initial map and basis for understanding who we are as people. Languages and cultures, contrary to what the literature might suggest, are not merely commodities or impediments. Languages and cultures form the basis of development for our intellects and the understanding of ourselves and the natural world. The meeting of cultures and the challenges we face collectively as human beings compel us to consider the type of education I have described. Our languages and cultures were the basis of our continuance as tribal peoples. They continue to be the creative force for our future in this shared space (Bouvier 1993).

We need desperately to embrace a view of the world that creates a shift of thinking about our existence, so at the very least we can control the despair of our own making. The purpose of education, then, is to help us to live in this world with others and to live in a way that does not destroy it, but preserves it, for those who follow us.

Cognizant of the challenges, we need to develop the gifts that each individual brings: linguistic abilities, cultural knowledge, affective development and creative action (Romero, 1994). As teachers, it means that we assume a participatory research stance in our work, that "we will make the road by walking" (Horton and Freire, 1990).

To develop the critical consciousness desired, we will need to situate our curriculum within the lived experiences of our students because it is affirming and validating. It means we are willing to critique the oppressiveness of being without work, the oppressiveness of colonization, the oppressiveness of experiencing racism, the oppressiveness of experiencing sexism and the oppressiveness of victimization.

Participants and Their Relationships

The strong emotional tie we have to community schools comes from participants and their relationships to each other. In a context of under-funding, effects of rapid change, relationships appear strained everywhere I travel. Past evaluations of community schools suggest, above all, the need to define roles and responsibilities clearly (Saskatchewan Education, 1984).

A critical factor needing our attention in relationships is that of authenticity. Authenticity as a foundation in relationships should reflect the quality of our being, rather than just the position or role we might hold. As we work together toward the vision, the emphasis must be on strengths that individuals bring to the process. The process must recognize the important role and contribution of every person. Relationships must be nurtured through honest communication, co-operation in undertakings, and through workable processes for decision making and for resolving conflict. Above all, community education development requires a willingness to accept change (Calliou, 1993).

This context, and contemporary understanding of knowledge and ways of knowing, requires each of us to be a teacher and a learner. The quality of this relationship should be family-like (Sergiovanni, 1993; Ramsankar and Hart, 1992). The core common human values we might promote are love, truthfulness, respect for life, wisdom, hospitality, sharing, generosity and peace (Kidder, 1994).

Children, parents and teachers must be involved in decision making. As teachers, our work with the community and particularly parents must move beyond "public relations" to meaningful dialogue and involvement. It is also extremely important that the adults working close to the children reflect the make-up of the community. Imprinting is important. Because staffing turnover is likely a factor, the revisiting of core values and purpose cannot be overdone. While the literature does not provide a foolproof recipe for community development and education, a process of involvement and advocacy are critical underlying factors, as is willing participation of all the participants. Studies in Saskatchewan have identified willing participation as an important factor, especially in the selection of teachers (Saskatchewan Education, 1984; Smadu, 1991).

Another factor that needs monitoring in relationships by all participants is the issue of dominance. Dominance by an individual or any group is not acceptable. Strong leadership to ensure that respect, democracy and fairness prevail is necessary. Both legally and socially sustained inequities in the end create injustice. We must be mindful that those most susceptible to a power imbalance are the people who are poor and the children themselves; it is important they have power and a voice.

The challenge issued in this section on participants and their relationships comes with an expanded definition of a locale. It includes people with central authority and decision-making power, along with the families and children who are the recipients of the program and the people who work in these communities. Where do the director of education, the trustees for a public board of education, the ministries of respective agencies who serve the people in the locale, the designated leaders in the education system, the minister of education and the premier of this province fit in this picture? What are their roles and responsibilities as legislators, as policy makers and as influential people with assigned authority?

Calliou (1993), challenges us to view participants and relationships beyond a human level, to include all life. I offer found words from the World Indigenous Peoples' Conference on Education (1993), held in Wollongong, New South Wales, Australia. The South American delegates challenged us to make the connection to land in our discussion of education. The words are as follows in a poem I wrote (Bouvier, 1999).

The Question of Land and Indigenous Education

land is power
land is transcendental
we cannot just talk
of land
we must reclaim it

land is a spiritual base
land is an economic base
we cannot just talk
of land
we must live on it
through our actions
we guarantee
an Indigenous education

the destruction of land
is the politic
we must address
to reclaim our knowing
to reclaim our cultures

education does not
have to be written
we must live it
it is community life
that nurtures
not government structures

land is the politic
we must address
internationally
Aski oma
peyakwon kimamanow[1]

Results Expected for Lasting Change: To Achieve Social Justice

Connell's (1993) definition of social justice has been adopted for this section. Social justice is the benefit – social, cultural, economic and political – that we accrue individually and collectively to benefit our living. It means that every person and group has equal right to the most extensive liberties, within a context of balance, for a like liberty for all (Wren, 1977). It requires consciousness and a capacity to change the conditions of our living. Hampton's (1993) 12 standards for emerging theories in Indian education informs this discussion further. One standard argues for relentlessness in the battle for our children. The war, he claims, is "between that which honours life and that which does not." These results will require activism, based on knowledge and wisdom. Sharilyn Calliou (1993) adds other outcomes which she broadly describes as a cohesive identity, self-determined change and community-based democracy. I have proposed that education fulfill a conserving capacity, a creative capacity and a critical capacity in a complex global community. To achieve these capacities, we will require a curriculum that is morally and culturally significant to a world community, with teaching centred on human imagination and story (Common, 1991).

Has our thinking about community schools changed? My exploration would suggest that I hope so. Relationships have evidently been fostered across cultural lines. We need to continue what we have started, to nurture it and to deepen it for all our children's sake. Education for social justice cannot be neutral, yet it must be just (Wren, 1971). My own experience suggests that shared power will not come easily or without pressure. Change to benefit people who are poor, a large segment of this population being Aboriginal people with a unique history and relationship to this land, will not be conflict-free.

I close with a story that involves the initial preparation of this work. The working title of this paper was "Good Community Schools Are Sites of Struggle." My choice of the word, struggle, created a long discussion with a friend. My friend, a male, believed it had a negative quality that did not embody the essence of what community schools were about. I agreed that it was a strong word, but I also believed it had positive connotations; meaning one would proceed with great effort for the educational needs and other needs of the community served by "community schools." Because I wanted the participants of the conference to listen to my message, I compromised. The original title was inspired by Herbert Kohl during a visit to Saskatoon promoting his book, "I Won't Learn from You." A man in our study circle shared his story of travelling world wide to find a good school; he had not found one. Wisely, Herbert Kohl responded with his own story to provide a good education for his children. He said, "What I did not understand then, is that there is no perfect school in an imperfect world. Today, I would look for the school where a struggle is taking place on behalf of the children."

Notes

[1] Michif, meaning "the earth, it is like our mother."

References

Barlow, M., and Robertson, H.-J. 1994. *Class Warfare: The Assault on Canada's Schools*. Toronto: Key Porter Books Ltd.

Bouvier, Rita. 1993. "Critical Education for Aboriginal Youth: A Balance to Conserve and to Create." Presented to the 5th National Conference on Multicultural, Intercultural and Race Relations Education, 25-27 November 1993, Vancouver, British Columbia.

Bouvier, R. 1999. *Blueberry Clouds*. Saskatoon, SK: Thistledown Press Ltd.

Calliou, Sharilyn. 1993. "Toward Community: The Community School Model and Health of Sovereignty." *Canadian Journal of Native Education* 20, no. 1: 27-43.

Common, Dianne. 1991. "In Search of Expertise in Teaching." *Canadian Journal of Education 16*, no. 2: 184-197.

Connell, R. W. 1994 "Poverty and Education." *Harvard Educational Review 64*, no. 2 (summer): 125-149.

Connell, R. W. 1993. *Schools and Social Justice: Our Schools/Our Selves*. Monograph no. 12. Toronto: Our Schools/ Our Selves Education Foundation.

DeMello, Stan, et al. 1994. "Discovering Common Meaning - Planning Community Development Education with First Nations." *Plan Canada* (Jan./ Feb.): 14-20.

Freire, P. 1999. *Pedagogy of Freedom: Ethics, Democracy, and Civic Courage*. New York: Rowman and Littlefield Publishers Inc.

Horton, M., and Freire, P. 1990. *We Make the Road by Walking: Conversations on Education and Social Change*. Philadelphia: Templeton University Press.

Kidder, Rushworth M. 1994. "Universal Human Values: Finding an Ethical Common Ground." *The Futurist* (July-August): 8-13.

Hampton, E. 1993. "Toward a Redefinition of Native/Alaskan Education." *Canadian Journal of Native Education 20*, no. 2: 261-309.

Lamonthe, Rene. 1993. "Dene Teaching Methods." Prepared for the Royal Commission on Aboriginal Peoples by the Dene Cultural Institute and The Native Women's Association of the NWT.

Ramsankar, S., and Hart, Charles. 1992. "Creative Curriculum for an Inner City: A Case Study of Alex Taylor Community School. *Journal of Curriculum and Supervision 7*, no. 4: 334-348.

Romero, M. E. (n.d.). "The Keres Study." A paper based on the Gifted and Talented Research Project – Identifying Giftedness Among Keresan Pueblo Indians. Principal Investigators: M. E. Romero and Holger Schultz, Implementation 1990-1992.

Saskatchewan Education, 1984. Evaluation of The Community Schools Program; Amplified Report. Published by Saskatchewan Education, Regina, SK.

Saskatchewan Education. 1996. *Building Communities of Hope – Best Practices for Meeting the Learning Needs of At-Risk and Indian and Metis Students -* Community Schools Policy and Conceptual Framework. Regina, SK: Saskatchewan Education.

Saskatchewan Education, Training and Employment. 1993. Children and Families "At Risk": Demographic Trands and Risk Factors.

Sergiovanni, T. 1993. "Organizations or Communities: Changing the Metaphor Changes the Theory." Invited address, American Educational Research Association annual meeting, Atlanta, GA.

Sergiovanni, T. 1994. *Building Community in Schools*. San Francisco, CA: Jossey-Bass Inc. Publishers.

Smadu, G. 1991. "A Survey Based on Recommendations Made by the Community Schools Evaluations – A Report Presented to the Indian and Metis Education Advisory Committee." *Community Schools* (March).

World Conference of Indigenous Peoples on Education. 1993. *The Coolangatta Statement on Indigenous Rights in Education*. Wollongong, NSW, Australia.

Wren, B. 1977. *Education for Social Justice: Pedagogical Principles*. New York: SCM Press Ltd.

Chapter 4
On the Margins of the Middle: Aboriginal Girls in an Urban Middle School

Heather A. Blair, University of Alberta, Canada

Introduction

In urban middle-years classrooms, children are involved in the daily process of constructing their identities. Ethnicity and gender are two very important parts of this socially constructed phenomenon. This chapter is an examination of gender and ethnicity in a multicultural urban classroom where Aboriginal (Cree, Saulteaux and Métis), El Salvadorian, Chinese, Iraqi and Euro-Canadian (English, French and Ukrainian) early adolescent youth established their relationships. It is also about the connections between gender, race, ethnicity and class, and a discourse on how these constructs contribute to inclusion or exclusion. It is about the co-construction of the marginalization of Aboriginal girls.

An examination of these girls' lives illuminates the realities that many urban Aboriginal girls face in middle-years classrooms, as well as clarifying how positioning by gender and culture is an active social process that, in this urban context, served to reify the status quo.

Methodology

I have had to address many methodological questions and issues throughout this work. First, as a non-Aboriginal, middle-class, adult woman, I must continue to acknowledge my own stance and think about how I position myself in this research (Dyck, 1993). As a teacher and teacher educator with 20 years' experience in Aboriginal education, I have come to understand that the realities of the lives of Aboriginal children are different from the lives that I and my children experienced growing up white and middle class. While describing the experiences of the Aboriginal girls in this classroom, I

63

continued to consider the uniqueness of these girls as individuals. Although in some ways they appear typical of early adolescents, the Aboriginal girls were not a monolithic group. They constructed their gender and ethnic identities in varied and unique ways.

Over the course of one school year I visited the school, and Grade 8 classes, as a participant observer at least one day a week. I spent two weeks at the beginning of the year and the last week in the classroom, and attended all major events. I interviewed the girls about their life experiences and asked them what it was like to be a girl in this school. I tape-recorded their talk and recorded their interactions. I continued to look at what gender, race and ethnicity meant to these girls, with whom they identified and how they positioned themselves. I looked at the patterns of interaction between girls of different ethnic origins and tried to ascertain what aspects of this interaction could be attributed to their identity. I researched the composition of the community, went to community and school functions, hung out at the nearby 7 Eleven [a convenience store] before and after school, and observed the ethnicity and genderedness of these kids' lives.

Gender, Race and Class in Harbourview

Harbourview is a low-income community situated on the perimeter of a small, mid-Western Canadian city. In communities such as Harbourview, many issues of gender exist, such as teen pregnancies, single parenting and abuse (Blair, 1996, 1998; Blair, Rolheiser and Reschny, 1995). Over the years, girls from this neighborhood have been relatively successful in terms of grades in elementary school and high school, but they have not generally continued on to post-secondary education. A good number dropped out of high school, started families at an early age and live below the poverty line. Others end up in low-paying traditional jobs or stay at home as homemakers and caregivers. There are also girls from Harbourview who never live to adulthood and whose lives are taken either by themselves or others through extreme acts of violence.

Gender divides the population of Harbourview in a number of ways. Family life, public life and the work place are obviously gendered. Women continue to tend to work in the service industries and professions such as teaching and nursing, whereas men tend to work at a wide range of professional and blue-collar jobs. Men still earn more than women in Harbourview, as they do throughout the city and the country. Nationally, women in Canada earn only 62 percent of what men earn (Canada, 1996).

This western-Canadian city has another division, which is geographical as well as a demarcation of class and ethnicity. There is an "east side" and a "west side" to the city, clearly marked by the river. This construct, east side vs. west side, has existed since the east side was settled as a temperance [alcohol-free] colony, and the non-temperance west side developed across the river from it. To this day, the east side is thought of as the more prestigious place to live, with the university and many of the city's wealthy homes located there. The west side is more culturally diverse and less affluent. Harbourview is on the west side.

The west side has been the home to more recent immigrants for many years. The Chinese community, for example, has a very visible presence here, with Chinese restaurants, grocery stores and a home for the elderly. The Cantonese and Mandarin languages are spoken in these places, and Chinese newspapers and notices indicate that it is a significant written discourse as well. Chinese men and women are employed in these businesses, which are primarily Chinese owned.

The Ukrainian immigrants also originally settled on the west side. Even though they now live throughout the city, they still have a strong presence here. It is not uncommon to hear the Ukrainian language spoken in stores and community centres; however, evidence of it as an authentic means of written discourse is uncommon. Several older suburbs in this area are home to many elderly Ukrainian people. There are two butcher shops, several bakeries, a Ukrainian restaurant and a giftware store. These businesses are owned either by men or husband-and-wife partners and employ both men and women. The women tend to be employed on a part-time basis.

The west side is where many of the Aboriginal people in the city live. A number of community services serve primarily an Aboriginal clientele. For example, the Indian and Métis Friendship Centre provides community, social, recreational and cultural services. The Aboriginal people on the west side tend to be poorer than their European or Asian counterparts and have lower levels of education and higher rates of unemployment. They often face problems related to housing, racism, lack of employment and health. There are many single mothers among this group and few opportunities for employment. Aboriginal languages are spoken in some homes and in such public places as the hospital and the drug store; however, no print in any Aboriginal language is found in public places.

Situated on the west side, the community of Harbourview has further demarcations of gender, race and class. Harbourview Road, for example, divides the community into two parts. On one side of the road are mostly apartments, and on the other side houses. The apartment buildings are home to many Aboriginal people as well as unemployed and working-class non-Aboriginals. Some residents in these apartments are students at the community college or Aboriginal post-secondary institutions. Others are single mothers working in their homes and raising their children or going out to work part-time.

The residents of the houses are also predominantly working-class families, although they are somewhat better off financially than the apartment dwellers. There are more households with two adults, more two-income families and fewer Aboriginal homes. There is less mobility among the families in the houses than among the families in the apartments, even though some of the houses are rented. In 1993 the population of this community was 4740, with 973 of these being children of elementary-school age. There were few elderly people in the area, and, in fact, less than 10% of the population was over the age of 50. The average annual family income was $36 886 (Canadian) in 1991, yet 28.3% of the families earned $19 999 or less and 11% less than $10 000 (Saskatoon, 1993). These families were poor.

Gender, Race, Ethnicity and Class at St. M. School

St. M. School, situated in the middle of Harbourview, is part of the local Catholic School Division. During the 1994/95 school year, St. M. school had about 500 children in kindergarten to Grade 8. Approximately half were girls, and at least one third were of Aboriginal ancestry. There were also another 10-15% Asian, Filipino, East Indian, Middle Eastern, South American and African children. There were 20 teachers, eight teacher assistants, a principal, a secretary, a part-time social worker/counsellor, a part-time librarian and a part-time Aboriginal liaison worker. The school staff did not reflect the student diversity. For example, only two teachers on this staff were of a minority culture, and they were both Métis men.

The school staff realized that the student population was becoming more diverse but were uncertain as to what it meant for their classrooms and school. Over the year little was done in the school to validate cultural diversity and to accommodate the different perspectives or experiences of these children. Few discussions acknowledged the impact of culture or gender on the children. As Ellesworth (1994) suggested, it was assumed that the norm was a "white, heterosexual, Christian, able-bodied, intelligent, thin, middle-class, English-speaking and male" (p. 321) child.

At the onset of this study, 18 girls and 12 boys were in this Grade 8 classroom. The numbers changed as new students arrived and others left part way through the term. By the end of the study two girls and one boy had left. Thirteen of the remaining students were of Aboriginal ancestry, as were all three who had left. There were two Asian boys, one Canadian born and one who had been in Canada for over five years. There were four adolescents who were new to Canada in the past five years: one girl from Central America, two boys from South America, and a Middle Eastern girl who had just recently arrived in the country.

The Girls

The girls in this classroom were busy adolescents, curious and involved in the world around them. They came from eight different ethnic groups (see Table 1), and friendship groups were strong.

Friendships were of obvious importance among the girls in Grade 8. Core friendship groups formed early in the year, some carried over from previous years, and several girls moved between friendship groups. Doris explained it by saying, "Cause girls, they're like, they're friends with one group, and then they're – a girl will get mad at each other, and then they're friends with another group."

Table 1 represents the girls in the classroom by ethnicity and core friendship groupings. The term *chick* used here was often used by the girls when referring to each other and was used as a kind of compliment or statement of inclusion. It was not used in a derogatory way.

Interactions between boys and girls were an important part of this Grade 8 class. Flirting, teasing, arguing and ignoring were obvious between the girls and boys on a daily basis. Still, the friendship groups remained single gender. The girls said they "hang out with the guys" after school hours, but the classroom groupings were usually either girls or boys. Some of the girls' friendship groups were

Table 1
Girls' Ethnicity and Core Friendship Groups

Name	Ethnicity	Friendship Groups
Annette	Cree	4
Carla	Saulteaux	1
Carol	Anglo-Canadian	2
Cindi	Anglo-Canadian	1
Diane	French-Canadian	2
Denne	El Salvadorian	2 / 4
Doris	Anglo-Canadian	1
Jamie	Cree	4
Janelle	Métis	2 / 3
Jerline	Métis	3
Korrine	Iraqi	5
Shannon	Anglo-Canadian	1 / 2
Sheena	Métis	3
Tanis	Cree	1
Toni	Ukrainian/Canadian	2 / 3
Trish	Ukrainian/Canadian	1

Note: The girls are categorized by numbers representing the four main friendship groups and the one single member group. 1 = the cool chicks; 2 = the straight chicks; 3 = the happening chicks; 4 = the invisible chicks; 5 = the ostracized chick.

multicultural; however, there were several Aboriginal girls who were not part of the rest of the girls' social interaction on any regular basis throughout the year. It became very obvious in this room that gender and separation by gender played an important role. However, this was not the only deciding factor. Race and ethnicity in combination with gender accounted for salient grouping determinants.

The "cool chicks" – Cindi, Tanis, Carla, Doris and Trish - were the most popular girls. They had been friends for several years, had helped each other in and out of school, and believed friendship was one of the most important parts of being a teenager. Cindi was of Ukrainian ancestry and had lived in Harbourview since birth. She was exceptionally outgoing and had lots of ideas and energy. Carla was very conscious of being "cool" and being a teenager. She had a real affinity for music and loved to sing and dance. She had been born on a reserve in Saskatchewan but had never lived there and had no recollection of visiting there. Tanis, in contrast, moved and spoke in a very quiet manner. She had moved here as a child from a neighboring province and went back regularly to visit relatives on reserves and in small towns. She was a very private person whose interactions were primarily among her group of friends or on a one-to-one basis. Cindi was the class valedictorian at their Grade 8 graduation, and Tanis and Carla led the singing of "The Rose" to a packed auditorium of family and friends.

Doris and Trish, both non-Aboriginal girls, were the "jocks" of the class. Trish took her school work and her sports very seriously. Doris was very active in all aspects of school life and frequently volunteered for school events. Doris and Trish were the girls in class who wore expensive sweaters, had team jackets, played in a city softball league, and had friends in more middle-class schools. At Grade 8 graduation they won the girls' athletic and all-round-student awards.

Shannon was everyone's friend and belonged to both the "cool chicks" and the "straight chicks." She, her siblings and her step-siblings had been at this school for most of their elementary years. All of the teachers knew Shannon and her extended family. Shannon would frequently comment in class on inequities she perceived in the world around her and saw herself as a helper and a negotiator.

The "straight chicks" friendship group included Carol, Toni and Diane. Carol came to St. M. school from the neighboring community of Briarpoint. She had friends in this class who, like herself, were non-Aboriginal but frequently hung out with the Aboriginal girls from the other Grade 8 room. Toni seemed young for her age and moved between the "straight chicks" and the "happening chicks." She did not fully belong to any group. Sometimes she hung out with Jerline and Sheena, but other times she switched alliances to either Diane or Carol. Diane was a French-Canadian girl who did not say much out loud in class, but was very thoughtful and concerned about her relationships with her friends. She had friends in both Grade 8 rooms and liked to invite them to her home. She lived on an acreage, had a horse, loved to camp and did a lot of things most of the other girls would not have had a chance to do.

Sheena and Jerline, two of the Métis girls in the class, formed the core of the "happening chicks." They were often in trouble. They cruised the school and neighborhood and were frequently in disputes with other students and teachers. They frequently skipped class, and on one occasion they were both expelled for three days. Sheena was extremely tiny and thin for her age and could have passed for a child of 11 or 12. She was, however, very conscious of a teen image and experimented regularly with new makeup, finger-nail polish and hair color. Similarly, Jerline was very conscious of her teen image and liked to talk about what "looked good." Neither of these girls spent much time on school work, but they were verbally active in classroom interactions.

Janelle, the other Métis girl in the class, was very quiet and timid during class time, but socialized with a wide range of girls outside of class time. She moved between the straight chicks and the happening chicks. She often volunteered to help others, and she was the only girl to sustain a relationship with Korrine after the novelty of having a new student from Iraq wore off for the rest of the girls. Janelle had been at this school since kindergarten and was well known among the teaching staff.

Annette, Jamie and Denne, the "invisible chicks," were the very quiet ones. They never spoke out in large or small groups. They hung out together until Denne moved into a friendship group with the straight chicks. Annette was extremely quiet yet very observant of others. She had recently moved to this city from a Cree reserve about 150 kilometres away where she still had friends and talked often about going back to visit. Jamie had also moved to Harbourview from another community. Like Annette she had gone to school on her reserve as well as in other urban settings and had gone to several schools in this city prior to St. M.

Denne was absent from school a great deal and seldom explained herself. Some days she did not come back after lunch and might stay away for two or three days. She was very reluctant to talk about her childhood experiences in El Salvador and in the refugee camp in Mexico. Her family had fled from their home, and she said she wanted to leave the memories behind and forget them. She tried very hard, in her silent way, to fit into the Canadian context.

Korrine was never really accepted into any friendship group in the five months she was in this class. She had recently arrived at the school from Iraq and struggled to make friends. She spent a lot of time going out to the English as a Second Language (ESL) classroom or to help her little brothers in their primary classrooms. She spoke very little English, seldom engaged in classroom interactions, and was seldom engaged by others. Janelle was the only student who tried to talk to her or help her with her school work.

Few of these girls regularly spent a great deal of time outside of their west-side neighborhood. They primarily hung out in the nearby mall and roller rink and viewed themselves as west-side kids. They did, however, have connections with youth in other places. Many had been to several schools, both urban and rural, and some to reserve schools. Many had siblings in high school, and they knew teens from the neighboring non-Catholic school. The girls all had dreams and aspirations for themselves, and most saw themselves as growing up and leaving Harbourview.

The Intersections of Gender, Race and Ethnicity

Gender and ethnicity emerged as interwoven constructs in this middle-years classroom. They were fluid, active processes, not static, clearly defined entities. These young adolescents were participants in the process of constructing their ethnic and gender identities through their face-to-face interactions with each other, the boys and the teachers.

West and Zimmerman (1987) suggested that gender is not a passive entity and that we all "do gender." They discussed gender as "an emergent feature of social situations: both as an outcome of and a rationale for various social arrangements and as a means of legitimating one of the most fundamental divisions of society" (p. 126).

Similarly, Thorne (1993) pointed out the salience of gender in North American society and said, "Gender is a highly visible source of individual and social identity, clearly marked by dress and by language; everyone is either a female or a male"(p. 34).

The gender groups at St. M. school were obviously divided into two gender categories, boys and girls. Physical appearance, clothes and adornments contributed to the definition of the groups. Although both adolescent boys and girls primarily wore blue jeans or corduroy jeans, sweat pants, or shorts, there was some variation among the T-shirts, plaid shirts and sweat shirts. For example, the girls sometimes wore short T-shirts, but the boys did not. Another marking was footwear. The boys almost always wore runners, whereas the girls wore runners, sandals and other flat shoes. Some girls wore necklace chains, pendants and rings, and all had one or two holes pierced in their ears. Some kids from each group wore watches, but the size and shape was specific to their gender. Quite a few girls wore rings, but few of the boys did. Gender in the classroom was only partially marked by these obvious physical realities. There were other features less obvious.

Cahill (1986) discussed the social nature of the process of constructing gender, and suggested that children are "recruited" into the categories of gender at an early age and learn to behave accordingly. During the process children begin to monitor their own and each other's behaviors regarding these gender categories. Garfinkel (1967), in his longitudinal study of a person going through a sex change, explored gender transformation and showed the kinds of involvement and the agency humans have in gendering. He said that gender identification is an arrangement of co-construction and that gender is a construct created through a complex set of routinized interactions; at the same time, gender also determines and structures the interaction.

Gender was central to daily life for these Grade 8 girls. The co-construction of gender was happening all day and every day. Gender images, gender boundaries and gender separation brought a multiplicity of realities to the process of gendering.

Racial and ethnic boundaries were also in play in the classroom interactions. For example, on most occasions when the students were asked to pick their groups, two of the Cree girls, Annette and Jamie, worked together. The one person who occasionally joined them was the El Salvadorian girl, Denne, who, towards the end of the year, had moved to a new group of friends. Denne explained her own friendship changes over the three years that she had been in Canada and in this school. At first she was friends with "the girls from other countries"; then with two of the Cree girls; and, lastly, with a group of Métis and non-Aboriginal girls. Her repositioning in friendship groups paralleled her acquisition of the English language. When she arrived at this school she spoke little English, and three years later was articulate enough to discuss a Stephen King novel she had read.

However, Annette and Jamie's position in the classroom remained quite constant. They were on the margins. Even when the teacher placed them in other groups for class discussions and activities, Annette and Jamie would physically position themselves on the outside of the group. They would sit just a little behind the others on a desk outside of the circle and would not move in close enough to take part or be expected to interact. Physical proximity was a very powerful tool for inclusion or exclusion. It was not as though others intentionally excluded Annette and Jamie; it was co-constituted and co-constructed, but never discussed.

As Cree youth, Annette and Jamie did not see themselves reflected in the classroom activities or school curriculum. Their lived experiences were not validated as being of importance in the classroom context. They were the only two girls in the classroom who had lived on a reserve for any extended period of time. They were more identifiable as Aboriginal kids than the Métis girls, for example, and they had many connections to the Aboriginal world. Their more traditional communication patterns (Heit, 1987) were not recognized by the others, and all of these contributed to the co-construction of their marginalization. Perhaps there was agency in their resistance to move in from the margins.

The girls who left the class part way through the year were also both Aboriginal girls, one Métis and one Cree. They both had experienced incidents of violence. One had threatened another girl in the classroom and had been expelled. The genderedness of the act was discussed by both students and staff, but no mention was made of the racial nature of the infraction. The second girl had had an incident of violence committed against her before she came to the school and had to go back to her reserve community for the legal proceedings. Neither of these Aboriginal girls returned to the school.

Language is thought to be another key element in the constitution of one's identity. Urciuoli (1985), citing Geertz (1973), suggested that "identity with a language community is ideologically important, a way of maintaining a sense of cultural rightness and orientation in the face of challenging conditions, particularly in the face of imbalanced and difficult external sphere relations with white Anglos" (p. 371).

Harbourview is located in a community of Chinese, Ukrainian, Dene and Saulteaux speakers on the city's west side. As discussed earlier, these communities have active speakers who use these languages on a daily basis. However, in St. M. school the English language was the only language ever heard outside of the ESL classroom. There were several girls in the "Tansi" middle-years Aboriginal culture group who indicated that they spoke Cree or Saulteaux, but these languages were never spoken in the school. The absence of Aboriginal languages was evident as well at the Tansi potluck and social held one evening at the school. When the drummer gave a prayer in Cree, everyone listened attentively; however, none of the girls used the Cree language throughout the evening. Aboriginal languages, like life experiences, were peripheral to the school and the classroom.

Although apparent constructs at work in the classroom, gender, race, class and ethnicity were seldom talked about in this classroom or school. These were silent boundaries that were not discussed and never openly questioned.

Constructing and Deconstructing the Complexities

Gender and ethnicity were woven together in a complex fashion. What it meant to be an Aboriginal girl in this classroom was not the same as being a Ukrainian-Canadian or an Anglo-Canadian girl. Neither was it the same for the Cree and Métis girls. There were overlaps, common experiences, but there were also points of separation and differences. Examining the following micro-social processes involved in classroom interactions helped elucidate some of the ways that these constructs, gender and ethnicity, were constituted. Three social processes, flirting, fighting and bugging – emerged as important to the girls in terms of their ethnic and gender identities. I would posit that these all contributed to the co-construction of the marginalization of the Aboriginal girls.

Flirting

The girls were very conscious of how they positioned themselves in relation to the boys. The cool chicks and the happening chicks engaged more frequently with the boys than the others. In the 1998 study, I discussed Cindi, who often went over to the boys' desks, particularly those of Mark, Derek and Morris. These were three of the most verbal and interactive "guys" and all were quite popular. Cindi teased them, laughed with them and then she would move back to her desk, often looking over her shoulder and talking as she went (p. 12).

By her own admission, "I'm a big flirt." Flirting to Cindi (C) was described as follows:

C: *Going up, hugging them, giggling with them, laughing at all their jokes – comments like: "Good comedy, – like,...I love doing it!" [laughs] (Blair, 1996, p. 85)*

Tanis' flirting was constructed differently from that of Cindi and was engaged in from a greater distance. Similar to Philips' (1972, 1983) analysis of interactive styles of the Warm Springs Native American youth, proximity and gaze were important aspects of

Tanis' communication. Tanis described flirting as, "If you're, like, sitting in a room, like, they're across the room, and you're – you just stare at them, and they look at you, and you just smile and then look away, and then do it again, and then again, and..."

Flirting was an important aspect of gendering for these adolescents. It was an important practice in the construction of gender. It was routinized to a great extent but differed among the girls, as Tanis and Cindi described. Flirting also operated to bring oneself into or to stay out of the cross-gender interaction. Some of the girls openly flirted. The "invisible chicks" – Jamie, Annette and Denne – by contrast, never engaged with the boys in this way. They avoided the boys, never approached them and, in fact, walked out of their way to avoid them. They kept a physical and interactive distance.

Engaging or not engaging in the social process of "flirting" seemed to carry with it communication patterns of a cross-cultural nature. Flirting was co-constructed between the boys and girls, and flirting behaviors may have reflected some of the communication patterns from their ethnic communities.

Fighting

The girls at St. M. school were very conscious of their behavior around other adolescents. Cindi described her own differentiation of behavior with regard to boys and girls and discussed how she would interpret a situation and act accordingly:

> *Like, when you're in a mall, and if there's a guy there, you try and act good, or something, or if there's a girl there, you like, walk solid, or something like [laughs] that – you try to be tougher...well, unless you're scared of that other group, or whatever, that you just, kind of look away and talk to your friends, and...keep on going.*

Although there were occasionally altercations among the girls, they weren't physically rough with each other in the classroom. In my 1998 study, I described that "it was not uncommon within friendship groups to see them combing each other's hair, draping their arms over each other's shoulder, or fixing something on each others' clothes" (p. 12). At the same time they were not adverse to being called "tough." Many spoke of fights that they had either been in or observed. Some of these fights had originated at school but took place outside of the confines of the school; others had nothing to do with school. Many of the girls believed that there were times when fighting was necessary. There was little question that this fight-

ing was gendered. It was primarily among girls. Fighting with the
boys was mostly verbal and will be discussed later in this chapter.

Eckert (1988), in her work with two groups of teens in a Detroit
high school, "Jocks" and "Burnouts," also found this value of an
image of toughness as salient to adolescent girls. In her study the
Jocks were concerned about a pure image, whereas the Burnouts
were proud of their "toughness and urban ties" (p. 205).
Interestingly, at St. M. even the more Jock-type girls valued toughness. Doris (D) and Trish (T) made the following comments:

> D: *It's just kind of, you just, you just show that you're not scared,*
> *kind of thing.*
>
> T: *Yeah, like: "Oh, I can fight her."*
>
> D: *Don't act scared, cause if you act scared, it doesn't...*
>
> HB: *Just makes it worse?*
>
> T: *Uh-huh.*
>
> D: *But don't, it's like, you have to, not act too tough? Because, but you*
> *can't act scared. You have to be in between. [Blair, 1996, p. 87]*

The girls talked about finding a balance between tough, scared
and safe. For the cool chicks and happening chicks, it involved more
face-to-face interaction in class and outside, even if at a distance. For
the invisible chicks, their limited face-to-face interaction with both
boys and girls in the classroom positioned them out of reach of altercations, yet they talked about fights in which they were involved
outside of the school, and it was obvious that they too valued
"toughness" in other contexts.

Bugging

As the boys and girls interacted in this middle years classroom,
they all contributed to the ongoing construction of who they were as
boys and girls. This process was not without tensions and conflicts.

In the girls' terms, "Those boys were bugging us" meant gendered conflict. When the classroom was quiet with independent
work, the tension was less apparent. However, times of class or
activity change, recess and lunch hour were prime times for conflict.
It manifested itself in physical as well as verbal interactions. Physical
conflict was evident in the ways the boys and girls moved in relation
to each other and in the kinds of physical contact between them. The
verbal conflict was both public and private. Terms such as "bitch,"

"slut" and "tight-ass" were directed at the girls by the boys, and the girls responded with "fag" and "You're gay."

The extent of the tension and conflict between boys and girls in the classroom was disclosed when I walked into the classroom one day during the teacher's absence to witness five Grade 8 boys surround, repeatedly bully, verbally abuse and hit Janelle while she pleaded with the perpetrators, "Don't! Please! Stop!" They didn't stop until they realized that an adult was present. This incident provided the teacher with an opportunity to inquire into the nature of "bugging." The students talked about the verbal and physical abuse taking place in the school, and the teacher initiated discussions and developed a unit of study to address the issues.

The three girls who received the least of this harassment from the boys were the invisible chicks – Annette, Jamie and Denne. They had even less interaction with the boys than they did with the other girls and, as a result, appeared to be spared this verbal and physical abuse. Their position on the edge had in some ways protected them. It was as though they implicitly knew this and made their interaction choices accordingly. This compares to a survey of high school students in this same school system the following year in which the girls who reported the least harassment and abuse from boys in school were the girls at the all-Aboriginal high school.

The two girls who were most often bugged were two Métis girls. Sheena, who was very small, reacted by fighting back, both physically and verbally, which often got her into trouble with the teachers. Janelle, by contrast, kept silent about the harassment. Her victimization reflected a double edge; she was silenced. The harassment of these two Métis girls in this class, perpetrated by boys but facilitated as well by the action or non-action of the other girls, provided one more window on the demarcations of gender and ethnicity at work in the school.

Summary and Conclusions

Heath and McLaughlin (1993) suggested that "ethnicity has always and everywhere been a series of creations brought about by the situations through which individuals or groups move" (p. 16). West and Zimmerman (1987) maintained that everyone is in the process of "doing gender." In this classroom these middle-years kids were actively engaged in weaving these processes together. The varieties and intersections of these constructs were unique to girls and groups.

The marginalization of the invisible chicks – Jamie, Annette and Denne – was a co-constructed phenomenon. Their quiet and distant presence provided few opportunities for their classmates to engage. They positioned themselves out of reach of their classmates, perhaps because it was a place of safety. Jaime and Annette remained insular in the process of constructing their gender and ethnic identities. Because this research did not involve experiences outside of the school, it was not possible to see these micro-processes at work elsewhere in their lives.

Denne was, by her own admission, reconstructing her world from that of an El Salvadoran, new to Canada, to a regular Canadian teen. Over the three years she had been here, she had repositioned herself, moving from being extremely marginalized as an ESL student to being a more central, "straight girl" in this classroom.

The happening chicks – Sheena, Jerline and Janelle – were more active in this process in the classroom and were more at risk. As young, urban, Métis women, they knew how to negotiate a mixed ethnic community and had many experiences with integration. In their co-construction of gender and ethnicity in this classroom, they too were marginalized, as was evident through the harassment. Although these girls were friendly and interactive with both the cool chicks and the straight chicks, no one intervened on their behalf when they were "bugged" on an ongoing basis.

The straight chicks – Carol, Toni and Diane – as a less racially and ethnically diverse group, seldom took part in the micro-social processes of flirting, fighting and bugging at work in this classroom and in the school. Their construction of themselves as "white" girls positioned them in a comfortable spot, and their more limited cross-gender and cross-cultural interaction kept them at a far lower risk.

The cool chicks, as a mixed ethnic group, were actively engaged as "with-it" teenagers. They were the most popular with the boys and created their gender and ethnic identities in collaboration with each other. They actively participated in both the flirting and fighting in the classroom and, though not generally the targets of the bugging, they were, by virtue of their compliance, party to the marginalization of the happening chicks.

This is not to say that the cool chicks were spared the ethnic and gendered realities of marginalization in Harbourview. For example, two years after their Grade 8 graduation, the lives of the two most popular Aboriginal girls in the class, Carla and Tanis, the only two who belonged to the cool chicks, were radically altered. One dropped out of school at age 16 as a single mom, and the other took her own life in quiet desperation.

The complexities of interaction in a middle-years classroom must not be overlooked. The margins are very powerful realities for Aboriginal girls in school today, and these realities need to be recognized and better understood. Ward (1990) discussed these realities for African American girls. She suggested that growing up black dictates the necessity of negotiating discriminatory and oppressive conditions. It means having to face daily injustice inflicted simply on the basis of skin color. It means having to live among and interact with people who may seek to hurt you (p. 219).

Similarly, Epp and Watkinson's (1997) edited collection of articles explains the complexities of violence in schools for Canadian girls and women. Yuzicapi (1997) in this volume discussed her experience growing up Aboriginal in western Canada and raised these issues for Aboriginal youth in schools.

The margins of the middle manifest themselves in many ways. They are constituted through both micro and macro processes. The micro-processes discussed in this chapter, the agency of all participants, the role of gender, race, class and ethnicity, and the need for making the implicit explicit in such classrooms become more and more important as young Aboriginal women give up on school and life. As teachers we have an obligation to them to facilitate schooling in a different and more diverse way. We must raise our own consciousness about the construction of marginalization, find ways to assist all the youths in our classrooms in understanding the micro social processes in which they are engaged, and find ways to explore the complexity of these issues in our middle-years classrooms in authentic and meaningful ways.

References

Blair, H. 1996. "Gender and Discourse: Adolescent Girls Construct Gender through Talk and Text." Doctoral dissertation, University of Arizona, Tucson.

Blair, H. 1998. "They Left Their Genderprints: The Voice of Girls in Text." *Language Arts 75*, no. 1: 315-23.

Blair, H., Rolheiser, A. and Reschny, S. 1995. "Adolescent Girls and Classroom Discourse." *Learning from Practice: A Bulletin of Teacher Research 1*, no. 1: 21-25.

Cahill, S. E. 1986. "Language Practices and Self Definition: The Case of Gender Identity Acquisition." *The Sociological Quarterly 27*: 295-311.

Saskatoon. 1993. *Neighbourhood Profiles*. Saskatoon, SK: City of Saskatoon, Planning and Construction Standards Department, Community Planning Branch.

Dyck, I. 1993. "Ethnography: A Feminist Method?" *The Canadian Geographer 37*, no. 1: 52-57.

Eckert, P. 1988. "Adolescent Social Structure and the Spread of Linguistic Change." *Language in Society 17*, no. 2: 183-207.

Ellesworth, E. 1994. "Why Doesn't This Feel Empowering? Working through the Repressive Myths of Critical Pedagogy." In *The Education Feminism Reader*, edited by L. Stone, pp. 300-327. New York: Routledge.

Epp, J. and Watkinson, A. 1997. *Systemic Violence in Education: Broken Promise*. Albany: University of New York Press.

Garfinkel, H. 1967. *Studies in Ethnomethodology*. Englewood Cliffs, NJ: Prentice Hall.

Geertz, C. 1973. *The Interpretation of Cultures*. New York: Basic Books.

Canada. 1996. *1996 Census*. Ottawa: Statistics Canada.

Heath, S. B. and McLaughlin, M. 1993. *Identity and Inner-City Youth: Beyond Ethnicity and Gender*. New York: Teachers College Press.

Heit, M. 1987. "Possible Differences in Communication Styles between Indian, Metis, and Non-Native Peoples." *AWASIS 1*, no. 3: .

Philips, S. U. 1972. "Participant Structure and Communicative Structure: Warm Springs Children in the Community and Classroom." In *Functions of Language in the Classroom*, edited by C. Cazden, V. John, and D. Hymes, pp. 370-94. New York: Teachers College Press.

Philips, S. U. 1983. *The Invisible Culture: Communication in Classroom and Community on the Warm Springs Indian Reservation*. Prospect Heights, IL: Waveland Press.

Thorne, B. 1993. *Gender Play: Girls and Boys in School*. New Brunswick, NJ: Rutgers University Press.

Urciuoli, B. 1985. "Bilingualism as Code and Bilingualism as Practice." *Anthropological Linguistics 27*: 363-86.

Ward, J. 1990. "Racial Identity Formation and Transformation." In *Making Connections: The Relational Worlds of Adolescent Girls at Emma Willard School*, edited by C. Gilligan, W. P. Lyons and T. J. Hanmer, pp. 215-32. Cambridge, MA: Harvard University Press.

Weis, L. 1991. "Disempowering White Working Class Females: The Role of the High School." In *Empowerment through Multicultural Education*, edited by C. Sleeter, pp. 95-121. Albany: State University of New York Press.

West, C. and Zimmerman, D. 1987. "Sex Roles, Interruption, and Silences in Conversation." In *Language and Sex: Difference and Dominance*, edited by B. Thorne and N. Henley, pp. 105-29. Rowley, MA: Newbury House.

Yuzicapi, M. 1997. "Personal Reconstruction: When Systemic Violence Stops." In *Systemic Violence in Education: Broken Promise*, edited by J. Epp and A. Watkinson, pp. 183-89. Albany: University of New York Press.

Chapter 5
No Friends, Barely: A Voice from the Edge of Indian Identity

Carol Leroy, University of Alberta, Canada

Many researchers have attributed Native[1] students' difficulties in schools to mismatches in communication between Native children and their Euro-American teachers (e.g., Philips, 1983). Low rates of participation and achievement have been also attributed to active attempts by Native students to resist schooling as representative of a broader society that has oppressed their people (e.g., Wolcott, 1987). However, much of the research on communication and resistance among Native students has been carried out on Indian reservations, with relatively little attention paid to Indian and Métis students in urban areas. In addition, in a recent review of the literature on American Indian and Alaskan Native education, Deyhle and Swisher (1997) point out that "research on female American Indians,[2] within an educational setting is almost non-existent" (p. 132) even though drop-out rates are higher for Native girls than for any other group, including Native boys, and they are one of the highest risk groups in America for living in poverty. The relatively few studies that have accommodated the voices of Native girls indicate that major factors in their leaving school are difficulties in establishing their ethnic identities and "an accumulation of negative experiences, such as uncaring teachers and racism against Indians" (p. 133). Hence, when Native girls show low levels of participation in schools, this may be interpreted as a form of resistance to broader societal inequities (Ogbu, 1993), but it is also important to recognize the ways such resistance can be driven by "the overwhelming desire for human connection – to bring one's own inner world of thoughts and feelings into relationship with the thoughts and feelings of others" (Gilligan, 1993, p. 153).

The purpose of this chapter is to explore the complexities of relationships and school resistance by discussing the story of Shannon, a ten-year-old girl whose experiences were fraught with difficulties in relationships with others, and who struggled, largely on her own, to construct an identity that would enable her to draw on the strengths of Native people. Shannon participated in a qualitative study (Bogdan and Biklen, 1992) that I carried out in her fifth grade classroom in the inner-city of a western Canadian city. The research was initially designed to explore the nature of social interactions and literacy in the classroom environment. However, as the study progressed, deeper problems with respect to identity and relationships came to forefront of the inquiry, and I began attending more carefully to stories told by the children about their relationships outside of the school as well as within it. Shannon was one of the children who was not only eager to share experiences, but also insisted that I write about them on her behalf so that other people "can know my feelings" – particularly those people who may be in a position to offer support to girls like her. The discussion below is intended to open questions about the needs of Native urban children whose difficulties in constructing identities are compounded by poverty, dislocation and uncertainties with respect to one's relationships that characterize inner-city environments (Heath and MacLaughlin, 1993).

Family Background and Future Prospects

Shannon was a fair-skinned and blonde girl. She resembled her mother, whom she identified as "white." At the time of the study, she was living with her mother and older sister and brother in the inner-city. She said that her mother was of French ancestry and her father was Métis. She said her father was an alcoholic who had quit drinking when he had joined "A and E" and was currently living in another province with Shannon's stepmother and stepsister. Shannon said she had lived with him when she was younger but there had been allegations of abuse and so she was sent from his home to live with her mother again. Since then, the children had relocated several times with their mother, and Shannon had attended three different schools before entering fifth grade. Like many of the other inner-city children in her class, she often talked about moving again. At various times she spoke of going back to where her father lived, or moving with her mother to a new location so that her mother could be with a boyfriend. As with her classmates, her talk about relocation was often interwoven with dreams of a better life – dreams that, more often than not, remained unfulfilled.

Over the course of our conversations, Shannon expressed a variety of ideas about what she might do when she grew up. Not surprisingly, she expressed cynicism about marriage. She told me that getting married is "the stupidest thing to do" because "you break up more." When asked to clarify what she meant, she said that when she grew up she would live with a man instead of marrying him so that she would not be as sad when the relationship ended – an outcome that, to her, seemed to be inevitable. With respect to jobs, she initially said she wanted to be a social worker when she grew up, so she could "help kids" the way a social worker had helped her when she was younger. However, after social workers entered her home to investigate allegations of child neglect, Shannon said she did want to be a social worker any more, but would likely become a stripper, like her mother. Although she was only ten years old, it seemed that her visions of a better future were already constrained by what she had seen happen to people around her.

Frequent relocation would make it difficult for any child to establish ties with a community, but, according to Shannon, her mother's lifestyle as a stripper and drug user was also interwoven with a sense of exclusion from the community at large. It would be both unfair and too simplistic to assign the mother blame for Shannon's situation. Instead, it seemed that the mother was struggling with strong problems of her own and perhaps had long felt the weight of rejection herself. The following is what Shannon said had happened when the mother had gone to a priest to have her children baptized and he refused her request. This account is indicative of the theme of rejection that permeated her accounts of her life:

Carol: What did your mom say?

Shannon: "Screw you."

Carol: "Screw you"? She must have been mad.

Shannon: She didn't care.

Carol: How do you feel about that?

Shannon: If they're, like, Christian, they want everybody else to be Christian. Cause they like to be Christian. And I ask lots of people that. And they go, "Yeah." And I go, "Would you like everybody in the world to be Christians?" "Yeah." Then why won't they let us be Christians?

Shannon's teacher expressed frustration to me that the girl insisted on telling her classmates what her mother did for a living, and even brought her mother's "promo picture" to school. The teacher was not judgmental about the mother, but she knew that when Shannon talked about her, this opened Shannon up to teasing from the other children, who wondered if her mother was a "hooker." From the teacher's perspective, Shannon was courting rejection from her peers. Yet, it seemed that, from Shannon's perspective, it was important to test her so-called friends to see if they, in contrast to others in the mainstream society, would accept her and her family on their own terms.

As discussed earlier in this chapter, resistance in schools is often attributed to children who experience alienation between their family's ways and those of the institution. Relatively little attention is paid to the possibility that resistance among inner-city children can be compounded by problems with relationships within the family. In this respect, Shannon spoke to me bitterly, not just about her separation from her father and the circumstances under which occurred, but also about times in which she had felt rejected by her mother. These times included incidents in which she said her mother had insulted her or put her down, and when her mother left her and her brother and sister on her own. When this happened, they sometimes went to stay with a neighbor who often took other children into her home. However, they were accused of causing trouble in this home, and so they were eventually "banneded" from it altogether and Shannon experienced this as yet another instance of being rejected by someone who might otherwise have cared for her.

Talking about what it was like to be left on her own, she struggled to express what perhaps is inexpressible: "I just pretend nothing's happening. Everything's fine in the family. I'm not scared. It's like, my life. Nobody else. Like, I know how to run it. And I'm not fine – I'm not – I'm not how's the word? Uh, scared." Sometimes Shannon tried to rationalize being left alone by saying that it afforded her an opportunity to become more independent. Yet, when the children were making Mother's Day cards, Shannon refused to make a card for her mother because "She doesn't deserve one." Then, when she thought she was going to be apprehended by social workers because of parental neglect, she said fiercely that she would "die" before she let them take her from her mother.

Being Native

Identity is the fact of "being a particular person" and community self-definition is an integral part of a distinctive collective identity or "being a particular group". (Saskatchewan Professional Development Unit, 1996, p. 10)

For Shannon, being Native,[3] like being Christian, opened up possibilities for belonging to a community that could lend her acceptance and support, but there was ongoing uncertainty was to whether these possibilities would be available to her. She said she knew that as a blonde girl and the child of a white mother, it would always be particularly difficult to establish her identity as a Native person in other people's eyes. She said the first time she had become aware of this was when she was about four years old and was visiting the home of a friend who was Native:

And, like, they thought I was White. And her mom goes, "Get out of my house. We don't allow White here." Right? And then I guess I started talking a little bit Native (with a Native way of speaking English). Like I am now, I think. And the mom goes, "Are you Native?" And I go, "Yeah."

It may have been with a teasing tone that the woman in this story had brought to Shannon's attention the need for her to play an active role in constructing a Native identity. However, Shannon did not have contact with her Native relatives, and she said she knew little about Native ways "because I don't know my Native grandma." She attended a school-based program for Native children to learn about their cultures, but, because of her moves between schools, she had only recently enrolled in the program. Even then, the children in this program met for only one-and-a-half hours per week, and this was not adequate for them to fully explore their cultural heritage. The result was that, for Shannon, constructing an image of Native traditions had become a matter of trying to piece together what she knew from various sources, including the streets.

For example, she emphasized that Native people are "tough" and rebellious because they used to "live free" and they had fought for that freedom, "Like the Iroquois – but Algonkians and Hurons and that. They, like, uh, they fought with the, uh, Iroquois, with the White." She also referred to this drive as being integral to her heritage: "My dad's Native. You know how, like, his parents and [their] parents and [their] parents. Like they had tough kids and tough kids and tough kids and that. So, I guess they – it just followed in the family or something." Métis writer Maria Campbell (1973) speaks of her own childhood in which the conversations of adults enabled her to connect the Native identity as "tough" with a strong cultural heritage and with collective political resistance. Shannon's social milieu did not afford her opportunities to explore what this notion of "tough" might offer her. Instead, she related the idea of being tough simply to one's ability to fight on the streets. She thought that Native people were good at fighting because "They have big muscles. That's how they were born." In Shannon's milieu, the girls frequently did engage in fighting, often over boyfriends. She was often heard to loudly threaten others, perhaps the aim of proving her toughness as a Native girl. However, she was a small girl who thought her size, in itself, meant that she would never be as tough as her Indian friends were. She emphasized to me, "Personally, I'm scared of full-Natives."

She also connected the idea of toughness to a willingness to engage in risky and destructive activities that were common among the people around her. One time, she told me about how Native people used to smoke "pot or something" in the old days, "And they passed it around in those pipe things. And they had a kid with them, so they passed the pipe to the kid." She went on to suggest that this is how "Native kids" start smoking cigarettes and marijuana today. That passing a pipe would be part of a sacred ritual was lost on Shannon. Instead, she saw smoking and taking drugs as something that distinguished Native kids from white ones because it was evidence of the toughness one had as being Native. She told me about a time she and an Indian friend were smoking and approached a young white girl, offering her a cigarette. The girl became frightened and fled, which Shannon took as an indicator of a cultural difference. Thus, courting the dangers of smoking became an activity that, for her, was a badge of ethnic identity.

She was also conscious of using language as a sign of her identity, often lapsing into a form of English commonly used by Native speakers in the local community. Yet, while she had successfully mastered the pronunciation and intonation that would mark one was an Indian, the subtleties of using language in a social context were seemingly unbeknownst to her. She often used language as an extension of her shows of bravado in the classroom, interrupting peers and the teacher, raising her voice and making demanding, rude or threatening comments. It seemed that this was her way of showing her toughness but, ironically, this use of language clearly marked her as White in the eyes of her Native peers. The latter girls emphasized to me that "It's not our way" to be "loudmouth" or "rude" or to use language to draw attention to one's self, the way that Shannon often did. They said they had grown up in families where one was expected to exercise restraint in speaking out – restraint that the Native girls said was not only traditional, but marked them as more mature than white children.

Indeed, even though the other Native girls in this classroom were well-known for their daring on the streets, in class they never caused disruptions, rarely spoke out of turn in whole-class discussions, never talked back to the teacher and refused to vie for attention through the variety of antics used by the white children. From their perspective, it was not "cool" to show excitement or become involved in trivial power games with the teacher in the classroom, nor was it consistent with their Native identities. Shannon seemed to be unaware of the role of her language in the distancing she experienced from the Native girls, although she said that no matter what she did, she would never be "full-Native." On the other hand, when asked what would happen if she talked and acted "white," she responded, "Most white people don't like me. So I think, well, if I was white I'd have no friends, barely."

Shannon and Her Teacher

In the literature on Native education, teacher-student relationships are often characterized as antagonistic, driven by some combination of the teacher's negative stereotyping of the children and the children's construction of the teacher as representing an enemy culture (Wolcott, 1987). This was not the pattern I saw in this classroom. The teacher had fierce opinions about the adverse affects of racism on Native children and viewed their cultural backgrounds as sources of strength for them. Indeed, with the students who were visibly Native she was often warmer, more respectful and more flexible than she was with the other children in this class. These children responded to her in kind and, even though they were often in trouble with adults outside of the classroom, in class they were invariably respectful and co-operative with this teacher. By way of contrast, with Shannon, there were no visible markers of Native identity to remind the teacher that she was in a vulnerable position with needs for acceptance that were just as strong as, or perhaps even stronger than, those of the other Native children.

When she first enrolled in this classroom she seemed to be eager to please the teacher, but she also had an inordinate need to have the teacher's individual attention. When her bids for attention were rebuffed, she responded by misbehaving and, over time, she became increasingly rude and abrasive. One day, she arrived to the classroom with freshly painted designs on the seat of her pants. She made loud remarks about the paint and then told the teacher she had to go to the bathroom to wash the paint off. When the teacher told her to remain in the classroom until after attendance was called, she stood at the front of the room, crossed and uncrossed her legs in an exaggerated fashion, and chanted loudly, "I'm going to piss my pants!" Even though I had spoken to the teacher about Shannon's problems, she believed that Shannon was struggling to obtain more power than a child should have in the classroom. In this particular instance, she gave in to Shannon, sighing, "All right, go then!" However, on other occasions she and Shannon engaged in extended arguments that ended with neither speaking to the other.

It was only when social workers investigated Shannon's home that it became clear to the teacher how strong Shannon's needs were. At this point, she wrote Shannon a caring letter and Shannon, who was thrilled to know the teacher cared about her, responded with gratitude and excitement and they began forging a relationship that, in this classroom, seemed to have come more easily between the teacher and the children who were visibly Native. Research on Native children's schooling often points to mismatches in communication as a source of problems in their education (e.g., Philips, 1983) and, more recently, researchers and theorists are highlighting pupil resistance to teacher authority as a central issue (e.g., Ogbu, 1993). However, as Deyhle and Swisher (1977) suggest, it is dangerous to conclude that Native children's cultural backgrounds and ethnic identities are barriers to their academic and social success. Instead, we need to remember that that a lack of contact with one's cultural heritage and a lack of support in developing ethnic identity may be the stronger problem. In Shannon's case, the difficulties in constructing a Native identity were embedded with problems within the family context, with repeated dislocation, with living in an urban environment that was filled with risks and with attending a classroom in which the teacher was unable to recognize her identity as a Native child.

There is increased awareness that Native children face extra barriers to success by virtue of their membership in a visible minority that still experiences inequity and racism. Relatively little attention is paid to the needs of children who face barriers in their attempts to make visible their memberships in those minorities. Like many other urban Métis and Indians, who are not visibly Native and whose ties to Native families and communities are weak, Shannon might have tried to develop an identity as white. However, as Campbell (1973) and Culleton (1983) depict in their stories of Métis girlhood, such identification is at the cost of locating roots that would enable the child to reclaim cultural strengths and traditions, and to reclaim a heritage of resistance. Shannon's attempt to draw on the strengths of being Native was, in a sense, political. But it was also personal, in that her relationships with her parents, her peers and her teacher all seemed to be driven by the search for strong and caring relationships that could support her growth and identity. The more these relationships remained closed to her, the more actively she worked to cling to them, in ways that remained largely unsupported by the adults around her. This striving to be in relationship might account for why school achievement and participation is often weakest among Native girls whose ethnic identity is weak (Deyhle and Swisher, 1997).

As Shannon's story shows, a Native girl's struggle to identify one's self in relation to a people and a history cannot be considered in isolation from a struggle to establish and maintain connections with one's family and community. In her case, resistance in a classroom was not the outcome of a girl's Native cultural background; instead, it seemed to be embedded in an emptiness caused by the loss of cultural connections.

Notes

[1] The term "Native" is used in this essay to refer to people who identify themselves as members of Indian, Métis or Inuit groups. Similar terms are "Aboriginal," which has political and legal connotations of claiming membership in one of these groups, and "Indigenous," which is a broader term referring to aboriginal peoples in the international context. The use of the term "Native" in this chapter represents the usage in the context where the study was carried out.

[2] Here, they seem to be using the words Indian and Native interchangeably.

[3] Note that Shannon did not identify herself as Métis, but used the more general term "Native."

References

Bogdan, R. C., and Biklen, S. K. 1992. *Qualitative Research in Education: An Introduction to Theory and Methods.* Toronto: Allyn and Bacon.

Campbell, M. 1973. *Halfbreed.* Toronto: McClelland and Stewart.

Culleton, B. 1983. *In Search of April Raintree*. Winnipeg: Pemmican Publications.

Deyhle, D., and Swisher, K. 1997. "Research in American Indian and Alaska Native Education: From Assimilation to Self-Determination." In *Review of Research in Education*, edited by M. Apple, vol 22. Washington, D.C.: American Educational Research Association.

Gilligan, C. 1993. "Joining the Resistance: Psychology, Politics, Girls and Women." In *Beyond Silenced Voices: Class, Race, and Gender in United States Schools*, edited by L. Weis and M. Fine. New York: State University of New York Press.

Heath, S. and McLaughlin, M. 1993. "Ethnicity and Gender in Theory and Practice: The Youth Perspective." In *Identity and Inner-City Youth: Beyond Ethnicity and Gender*, edited by S. Heath and M. McLaughlin. New York: Teachers College Press.

Ogbu, J. 1993. "Frameworks: Variability in Minority School Performance: A Problem in Search of an Explanation." In *Minority Education: Anthropological Perspectives*, edited by E. Jacob and C. Jordan, pp. 83-109. Norwood: Ablex Publishing Corp.

Philips, S. 1983. *The Invisible Culture: Communication in Classroom and on the Warm Spring Indian Reservation*. New York: Longman.

[SPDU/SIDRU] Saskatchewan Professional Development Unit and the Saskatchewan Instructional Development Unit. 1996. *Aboriginal Cultures and Perspectives: Making a Difference in the Classroom*. Saskatoon and Regina, SK: Authors.

Wolcott, H. 1987. "The Teacher as Enemy." In *Education and Cultural Process: Anthropological Approaches to Education*, edited by G. Spindler, pp. 136-50. 2nd ed. Prospect Heights, IL: Waveland Press Inc.

Chapter 6
Getting to Know Us

Linda Wason-Ellam
University of Saskatchewan, Canada

Mainstream schools are a mosaic of cultures, each part intended to be in balance while making a distinct and positive contribution to the whole. Classrooms, too, are a microcosm of society with children of diverse races, cultures and ethnic groups, including children of Aboriginal and Métis ancestry, working and learning in harmony. These children bring to school their language, values, beliefs and ways of learning. But not all schools are welcoming. Often, children are strangers in the natural rhythm of classroom cultures. This is true in inner-city community schools, which are often composed of children who live their lives in flux within the cycle of poverty and transience. Many children live in unbalanced home environments tempered by temporary guardianship, foster care, parents serving prison sentences, the cycle of addictions, transient life and the violence that often characterizes inner-city neighborhoods. In a postcolonial society, many urban Aboriginal and Métis families are experiencing ethno-stress (Cajete, 1994), a disruption in their cultural life and belief system, which negatively impacts on their traditional values and ways of learning. Since schools within the inner-city are often just footsteps away from bingo halls, saloons, pawn shops, or alcohol and drug treatment centres, they are not exactly areas where threads of community can be knitted and strengthened. Cultural identity may not be intact, since family life is often shattered in the struggle to cope with living in alienation and isolation in urban communities away from the networks of kin. Although many of these Aboriginal or Métis families do not practice their traditional ways, the cultural roots lie dormant waiting to sprout again.

Behind their outer facade, mainstream schools are beginning to develop a respect and appreciation of others. Although schools are not able to replicate traditional values and a sense of spiritual connectedness to the land when the earth beneath the children's feet is several city blocks, there is a growing sensitivity to the communication styles and participation structures needed to be more culturally congruent with students' own lives. To address this need, classrooms are restructuring their learning environments so that children can work together co-operatively in communities of learners rather than working in competitive or individualistic learning structures. It is assumed that co-operative learning becomes a positive safe haven and a trusting environment for children who are cultural outsiders or strangers to mainstream schooling.

Hanging Out in the Classroom

Working within several primary inner-city classrooms over an eight year period as a classroom ethnographer, I draw upon a kaleidoscope of impressions about how children connect to others in learning communities through language. By "hanging out" in these classrooms, I focused on the informal and formal language interactions between and among classmates. Language is an active process that reflects the power to create and shape reality. Perhaps the most vital aspect is that of social relations, because language sets up the positions that allow social interactions to occur. Children connect to classmates with a wide range of interactions and these interactions are used in different situations. I observed that, in the naturally occurring classroom routines, children often shared gossip and stories informally at the coat hook, or at work tables. This speaks to the role of context as increasingly important in educational research and theory building. Recent collaboration with anthropologists and other social scientists has broadened my appreciation for the importance of social-cultural meaning in ethnographic methodology. The increased value given to natural learning and authentic settings for research has helped me see how complicated it is to establish learning communities for children. What I saw was that informally connecting lives through narratives or stories can build connectedness to self and to others as it creates a classroom of affinity.

Strangers in the Classrooms

What makes inner-city classrooms problematic is that they are laced with uncertainty. School is often a revolving door as children change neighborhoods regularly, so that "no-one-knows-me" becomes the familiar pattern of relationship to others. For these children, school may not only serve as a learning community. It may be a haven of safety and belonging. The experience of being a stranger, an outsider, is a growing concern. We all experience being strangers at different times, and we become aware that strangerhood has many nuances. Children can be strangers as they enter in a new school or they can be strangers by virtue of their difference, whether it be physical, social, cultural, religious or racial. A child can be a stranger by remaining within herself or being at odds with the world. Whatever the situation, strangers live on the edge between their own world and the world of others that they have just entered. In inner-city schools, strangers by their presence ask something of us: they ask that their heritage or conditions be respected.

What invitations can mainstream teachers extend to strangers? Learning communities are the building blocks of cohesiveness in inner-city schools. To build a learning community, classrooms may focus on including cultural others in co-operative learning groups and setting a classroom environment that actively promotes dialogue, mutual care and respect for others. As Noddings (1992) reminds us, children need to be cared for in the sense that they need to be understood, received, respected and recognized. Often this is difficult. Cultural pluralism is written about but not yet lived. Communities of otherness rather than communities of affinity remain too often the patterns of classrooms.

How do we build a sense of affinity? Schools cannot replicate Aboriginal and Métis culture. However, inner-city teachers are grappling with exploring pathways for helping children within the classroom community enter into a collaborative relationship with each other. Creating spaces for others is not an easy task. In this chapter, I will address how personal stories shared in a classroom community allow children who are estranged from their culture make connections to self and to share in another's experience.

Storying Our Lives

Telling personal stories is a basic human activity of sharing news and remembering the past. It begins with the context of the family. Sitting around the kitchen table or gathering for a celebration, family members in all places and in all eras have entertained one another with anecdotes about recent events and old tales handed down from earlier times. The stories told became shared experiences and helped all to know who they were and where they came from. Why, then, tell stories in the classroom? Like a rap on the window, stories call us to attention. Through stories or narratives of personal experience, classmates discover what others have to teach them. In this way, positive peer relationships are built, other ways to communicate ideas develop, and, most importantly, the perspectives of others are more easily understood. But not all classmates are willing to view others in an egalitarian way or with affinity. Connecting lives through dialogue and interactions can create tensions, because inner-city communities are sites of individualism despite a emphasis on the sense of community within our culture. Individualism remains a dominant cultural model in our society economically and socially. To survive within the milieu of these neighborhoods, "you have to be tough and competitive. Fists and kicks go a long way to fostering a sense of self." To survive in school, children need to develop a social-self by talking and connecting in relation to others.

In traditional classrooms, children have few opportunities to initiate talk within classrooms. Recently, they have had a greater opportunity in small-groups to offer opinions, engage in exploratory talk and initiate new topics (Wells and Chang-Wells, 1992). Show-and-tell, sharing or talking circle (an Aboriginal participant structure flowing from east to west that ensures that all voices are recognized) are usually daily occurrences, but these activities are not always defined as a narrative activity. In these activities, each child takes a turn talking about an object or talking about an experience. Reluctance to speak or faltering attempts to articulate often leave some children squeezed out of many of these whole class activities. But class talk alone is not enough to help children connect. Stories offer more. Rather than organize whole class turn taking, children can participate in small conversational groups where stories are swapped. Wells (1986) recognizes that conversational storytelling or storymaking is an authentic structuring activity of sustained talk. Often overlooked as being trivial, conversational stories provide the ideal situation for the social communication. They provide contextual support that helps the child convey his or her meanings and grasp those expressed by others. Above all, it provides a real reason to interact with classmates and to design and creatively construct a message, anecdote or story in his/her own way. If given voice and honored, personal stories can become a powerful vehicle for bringing diverse voices into the classroom community (Wason-Ellam, 1995).

Intertwined with children's everyday lives are the stories they weave and hear told, stories they dream or imagine or stories they eventually would like to tell. In my research, I realized that stories provide children with a means of recounting and reassessing for others the mishaps and wonders of our day-to-day lives. When children converse, these everyday impromptu stories or "memory moments" enabled them to legitimize their sense of self as they attempted to make meaning of the experiences, beliefs and values of their own culture. From a myriad of sources are intertwining threads – memories, anecdotes, jokes, family stories, journeys, dreams, gossip and imaginations. Personal meaningful knowledge is socially constructed through shared understandings. This view of conversational storytelling rests on two assumptions about talk (Miller and Mehler, 1994) :

• it is a pervasive and culturally organized feature of social life in every culture

• it is a major mechanism of socialization

Conversational stories are also compatible with culturally relevant teaching, a pedagogy that empowers students intellectually, socially, emotionally and politically by using their own cultural referents to impart knowledge, skills or attitudes (Ladson-Billings, 1994). On first impression, personal stories may seem like idle tales, for they are told in the course of everyday happenings. Alasdair MacIntyre, a moral philosopher, states (1981) "we all live out narratives in our lives...and we understand our own lives in terms of the narratives we live out. He believes that the form of narratives is appropriate for understanding the actions of others. Stories are lived before they are told – except in the case of fiction (p. 197)." Storytelling flourishes in the day-to-day moments of our daily life. We tell jokes, relate experiences, give explanations and talk about the things the things we do. Whenever we want to say something, anything, we format it in story to help articulate our thoughts, emotions and impressions. Storytelling is not a "stage performance" but encompasses our experiences and daily life. However, sharing personal life may not be natural for all children. In the beginning, the stories told in the classroom were often spliced from the social worlds of mass media and the toy culture with themes and language emanating from videos, television, soap operas and gendered toys – i.e., Barbie and Power Rangers or re-enacting violent and aggressive acts from video game playing.

Sherry's story was typical of the personal tales volunteered initially. An excerpt from my field notes describes the context.

Watching Sherry come through the grade two classroom door with her flowing red hair bouncing in rhythm to her long strides, brings a feeling of déja vu. With her freckled countenance and stellar smile, she is what I imagined Anne Shirley [Anne of Green Gables] to be – wholesome and bubbling with a joie de vivre. Taking off her heavy winter coat, scarf, and mitts at the coat hook, Sherry rearranges her clothes theatrically to create the desired effect – a staged entrance as she makes her way into the Sharing Circle to join her classmates. Although it may have been minus 30 degrees outside, she was wearing a knitted top that skimpily just covered her thin chest, leaving her midriff seductively exposed to just below her navel. Coupled with a pair of thin fuchsia pink palazzo pants, her attire seemed more appropriate for a weekend aboard a cruise ship – if one was a single twenty-year old – and out of cadence with the daily life of an eight year old in a class-room community [February 1996].

Anxious to share in conversational stories with me and three peers, the sunshiny countenance becomes grim as she begins a long-winded narrative account relating the saga of her parents' parting. Sherry expressed unhappiness that she had to leave the family home and her father's custody. She felt put out that she had to live with her mother, two siblings, and her mother's boyfriend, away from the material advantages provided by her father. She offers:

Sherry's Story

Once I used to live far from here. It takes a whole day to get there on the bus and its too far to drive. Do you know that my father is rich and we had lots more in our other place than here. We lived in a big house. I don't like it at my mother's. My Dad works in a hotel in and he gets lots of money. Lots of money to buy lots of things. We never have to wait to buy things. If I ask for something, my Dad says "sure" and buys it for me. Did you know he is really rich? My grandfather is rich too. Anything I want they will buy for me. My mother never does. She says she doesn't have the money. I hate it when she says it.

My mother lives with Brent, who is not very nice. I hate him. He is always going out and staying for a couple of hours. He's cheating on my Mom, cos he is seeing another woman behind my Mother's back. I know. And I told her about it and now she knows. He is no good. I hope she throws him out and he never comes back. I don't want him living with us. My mother is waiting until after they go shopping and he buys things before she throws him out.

I want my mother to marry my father. He has lots of money. I hate liv-ing with my mother. If she married my father, than we could all live together. I wish, wish, wish. I am going to make them get back togeth-er. My father will do anything I say.

When I grow up, I am going to marry a rich man. I am never going to get divorced like my mother. I am going to make my husband love me. I want to have nice clothes like Michelle. I can have my own car, and credit cards and things. Then I can buy things. Victoria does and she is pretty. She has lots of rich men.

Victoria is on my program (The Young and the Restless). I watch it every day when I come home from school. Sharon is on the program, too, and she is marrying Nick. His father is really rich. She is lucky. Cos she has her own car and when she wants another one, Nick will give it to her. Anything she wants, she will get. Nick used to like Amy and she was pretty. But Sharon is prettier so he is with her now. They won't get divorced because he thinks she is pretty.

I want to be pretty, too. If I am pretty, then I can become rich like Sharon. I want to be like her when I grow up.

Typically, Sherry, age seven, fuses the "back story" from her favorite soap opera so that the characters from television became an extension of her own circle of family and friends. She talked about them with familiarity, and followed their relationships by embedding them and their plots within the personal stories of her daily life. Intertwined throughout is the cultural message that to be attractive is to be evaluated by the male standard and that securing a male provider is a woman's role. For Sherry and her classmates, conversational stories were stories of beauty and involved descriptions of themselves, in pursuit of older males, wearing tight jeans, sleazy tops [belly button showing], dangling earrings, exposing "boobs" and wearing leather jackets.

Sherry and her friends relied on the media to construct images of reality. They told wistful stories revolving around Barbies, videos, make-up, soap operas and singer Shania Twain. Meanwhile, the boys fantasized stories that put strength and violence at the forefront and incorporated Power Rangers, Sega videos and wrestlers as iconic heroes.

Stories are not books. According to Jones and Buttrey (1970), stories belong to children's talk about themselves and their world, and their impressions of the adult world. However, many children were obsessed with embellishing their stories with language and themes mirroring the adult culture. Things were not working. What the classroom teacher wanted to achieve was to have children connect to something deeper, a sense of who they were as people. Intervention was needed to invite children along new pathways of self-discovery.

Eliciting Stories

Just setting aside a time for personal stories is not enough to help children tap the "memory moments" that stand out in their daily happenings. Stories had not surfaced easily, so I asked the children to travel with me back to childhood to look for forgotten moments. Naturally, I shared a string of mine. I thought of the ways Nature creates, and the wonders I had experienced, which became the seeds of some tales: making sandcastles in the sand and watching the tide melt the magical creations away, the loft in the barn where there was always a litter of kittens every spring, and the neighboring pond where I skated each winter along the little lagoons hidden by the tree branches. I would start each story with "I remember the time." Eventually, children turned to partners and simply talked for three or four minutes; they saw many "times" come to the surface. If they turned up a big memory such as a long trip, I encouraged them to look for the highlight. If what they remembered seemed too small to be a "story," I asked them to back up in time to what preceded the moment or to background information, so the moment's significance became clear. I encouraged the tellers to celebrate grand as well as small moments of childhood: building forts with tree branches, making dolls from scraps of fabrics, imagining being someone else, or helping someone who was in need.

In addition we had literary conversations where we talked about the ideas in the books we read. In dialoguing about stories, we took a writer's stance when commenting about the author's style or patterns of writing. Talking among ourselves, we discussed how authors elaborated on incidents or "memory moments" and expanded those ideas into a story. We talked and thought about how in Sparrow Song, Ian Wallace (1986) described how two children care for an orphaned bird, nurturing it through the summer, and finally setting it free. Within the layers of meaning is a story about love, forgiveness and the gift of life. Then I asked if the story reminded them of any experiences they had had and requested that they listen carefully to each other's memories. Few had cared for an orphaned bird, yet every child in the room made a connection to the story. Moments of discovery often filled our conversations. As Cajete (1994, p. 169) suggests, remembering "is a way to re-know and reclaim a part of your life."

Stories ran deep like a river. Stories forded cultural boundaries as a way of remembering, making sense of things, understanding what happens, and even predicting what might be. In their narrative construction, children came to know themselves. Communities of affinity are based on trust, the risk of sharing personal stories, opinions and feelings with others who may either support those ideas or put them down and ridicule the disclosure. Trust builds when children openly share personal stories and opinions, when encouragement is given and when verbal and non-verbal put-downs are eliminated. Once children know that a teacher and other peers can be trusted not to ridicule, and will also share or disclose personal opinions, more risks in expressing new ideas and feelings will be taken (Hill and Hill, 1990).

Learning to Value the Personal Tale

Chris

One day not long ago, I was at Keely Lake. It is a place I like to go because I go fishing with my Grandpa not far from the reserve. For the next two days, I paddled in my grandfather's canoe. We paddled all over the lake looking for fish. Sometimes we went out early when the cool was rising from the lake and you could see that it often covered the lake. Often we would hear the loon making its laughing call. Usually we could hear the fish jump. When we saw the ripples on the water, we headed in that direction hoping for fish.

Once, when we came to the edge, I was trying to catch a frog and I fell overboard into the lake. I saw a fish and I said, "cool." I tried to catch it with my fist but no luck, it swam away.

All my money fell out of my pocket. All I had was $20.00 and all my money was wet. But I managed to get it all. And I jumped out and walked to the cabin where I dried my money on the steps. My money was still good and I could use it. Later, my grandpa came back from the lake. I showed him my "washed money." He told me that even though money looks like paper, it is made of material and it will still be good.

I used my money to buy two videos.

When children share stories from their lives, they begin to open themselves to others, and perhaps nowhere are others more willing to come close enough to hear than when they are being told a story. Faithful listening means that we turn our attention to the words of another. We begin to imagine an event from the side of another person, to grasp his or her uniqueness. As I listened to Chris, it became evident that his grandfather was his mentor and soul mate, guiding him far from the violence and temptations of life in the inner city. Chris told stories of hunting and learning to read the ecological signs of the bush: the impending storm or the signs and sounds of autumn.

Conversational tales are stories of personal experiences. They are a way to shape and reshape our lives, relating what has happened or imagining what could have happened. Moreover, they are an important resource for acknowledging ourselves as cultural beings. Through stories, voices echo and intersect with others in a socio-cultural world. In this manner, the children in this inner-city classroom evidenced cultural membership both through their ways of crafting conversational stories and in the very content of their tales (Dyson and Genishi, 1994). Stories stand on the shoulders of other stories. Classmates took threads from Chris's story and spliced them into stories of berry picking with their Kokum (grandmother); or stories from their relationships to kinship and clan. The sharing of personal stories became "the glue that holds together a diverse set of community members, giving them a common language experience along with a deeper understanding of one another" (Trousdale, Woestehoff and Schwartz, 1994, p. ix). In sharing, there is a recognition of needs, relation and response (Noddings, 1992, p. 21).

Sherry

> Once, I was cooking supper with my Mom. While I was peeling carrots, my Teddy Bear slipped under the table. It fell from my lap. But I didn't notice he was gone. When it was time to go to bed upstairs, I didn't know where Teddy was. I looked everywhere through the house with no luck. I didn't know my Teddy Bear was under the table. I asked my mom, "Where is my teddy bear?"
>
> "I don't know. I guess you have to sleep by yourself," she said. I felt sad and lonely because Teddy was my friend. It was hard 'cos I loved my Teddy Bear.
>
> Later, when I was asleep, my mom found my Teddy Bear under the table. My mom bought Teddy Bear to me when I was sleeping and tucked him under the covers with me. In the morning, I found Teddy snuggled next to me. I said "Thank you, Mom. I love you, Mom."

Whenever it is necessary to report "the way it really happened," the natural impulse is to tell a story that recounts the actions and events of interest in some kind of temporal sequence. Sherry's story does more than simply outline a series of incidents. It places those incidents in a particular narrative context, thereby giving it a particular meaning. That is, narrative translates knowing into telling. How we "author" our lives through articulating who we are influences what we think, how we feel and what we do.

In the interplay of storytelling, the child not only discovers identities within him/herself but deep-running feelings as well. Eliciting memory moments such as Sherry's, establishes that even small experiences carry significance (Gilyard, 1995, p. 68); these experiences help us to see each other as individuals, and to realize what we might share in common. Telling one story triggers others. One tale reminds someone of their own, which may in turn remind others of more details from a previous one. Sherry's story triggered a number of "lost stories" – lost cats, lost bicycles, lost in the shopping mall – which filled the classroom with connections. The strength of Sherry's tale is that self-narrative becomes a self-reflective interpretation of her life experiences, which through personal storytelling creates meaning from the relationships in her lives, a giving of herself to others.

Children are all storytellers, and they are all listeners. Storytelling, used informally, creates bonds, increases listening skills and fosters communication between others. Stories help them make sense of what is happening around them and within themselves. As life becomes more and more complicated, stories allow children to stop and ponder and catch their breath at the same time as they fill them with release and wonder.

Telling stories and listening to stories enriches children in so many ways. Children become aware of the magic and importance of words; their imaginations, once stimulated, never fade; and they carry with them a treasury of memories which will have lasting benefits. Zipes (1995) states it is important to try to instil a sense of community, a self-reflecting and self-critical community, in children to demonstrate how the ordinary can become extraordinary. Children as storytellers can weave threads which create a network of affinity that brings a classroom community together. And they learn about "getting to know one another."

References

Cajete, G. 1994. *Look to the Mountain: An Ecology of Indigenous Education.* Durango, CO: Kivak' Press.

Dyson, A. H. and Genishi, C., eds. 1994. *The Need for Story: Cultural Diversity in Classroom and Community*. Urbana, IL: The National Council of Teachers of English.

Gilyard, M. 1995. *Storyteller, Storyteacher: Discovering the Power of Storytelling for Teaching and Living*. York, MA: Stenhouse Publishers.

Hill, S. and Hill, T. 1990. *The Collaborative Classroom: A Guide to Cooperative Learning*. Portsmouth, NH: Heinemann.

Jones, A. and Buttrey, J. 1970. *Children and Stories*. Oxford: Basil Blackwell.

Ladson-Billings, G. 1994. *The Dreamkeepers: Successful Teachers of African American Children*. San Francisco, CA: Jossey-Bass Publishers.

MacIntyre, A. 1981. *After Virtue*. Notre Dame, IN: University of Notre Dame Press.

Miller, P. J. and Mehler, R. A. 1994. "The Power of Personal Storytelling in Families and Kindergartens." In *The Need for Story: Cultural Diversity in Classroom and Community*, edited by A. H. Dyson and C. Genishi, pp. 38-54. Urbana, IL: The National Council of Teachers of English.

Morgan, K. L. 1989. "Caddy Buffers: Legends of a Middle Class Black Family in Philadelphia." In *Talk That Talk*, edited by L. Goss and M. E. Barnes, pp. 295-98. New York: Simon and Schuster.

Noddings, N. 1992. *The Challenge to Care in Our Schools*. New York: Teachers College Press.

Trousdale, A.M., Woestehoff, S. A. and Schwartz, M., eds. 1994. *Give a Listen: Stories of Storytelling in School*. Urbana, IL: National Council of Teachers of English.

Wallace, I. 1986. *The Sparrow's Song*. Markham, ON: Penguin Books.

Wason-Ellam, L. 1995. "The Storied Life of a Second Language Learner." *Canadian Children 23*: 14-19.

Wells, C. G. 1986. *The Meaning Makers*. Portsmouth, NH: Heinemann.

Wells, C. G. and Chang-Wells, G. 1992. *Constructing Knowledge Together*. Portsmouth, NH: Heinemann.

Zipes, J. 1995. *Creative Storytelling: Building Community, Changing Lives*. New York: Routledge.

Chapter 7
Coyote: Experiences as a District Consultant

Shauneen Pete-Willett, Cree,
Saskatoon Public School Division

Folks in town began to talk about that coyote that was hanging around. She was making folks change the way things were done. They had to lock up the hen house and tie up the dogs at night now. They had never had to do that before.

Coyote sits on the hill above the village, she scratches her ear with an elegant paw. Her belly growls and she smiles a tiny smile. Her ears twitch at the voices from the village down below, she yawns.

The Men's Bathroom – Or What is a Coyote Like You Doing in a Place Like This?

Have you ever walked into the men's washroom by mistake and had that feeling wash over you that you just don't belong there? I was 27, with four years of teaching experience in an alternative high school. I had been hired as an educational consultant for Indian and Métis Education for an urban school division. It was exciting, and this excitement kind of went to my head. I thought, "Hmm, I made it!" I bought a new suit, briefcase and got my hair cut. My dad gave me a huge coffee cup, "a conversation piece," he said, to help me make friends. I picked up that cup that day, straightened my skirt, re-applied my lipstick and strolled down the hall for a coffee. A smiling woman stepped into the hallway and spoke: "Oh! You're that nice new Indian girl we hired. My neighbor's an Indian – are you related?" I had that feeling that time, that I had walked into the men's washroom, and that I did not belong.

I had hoped that somehow people would know more about racial issues. I had assumed that, because in my former role as a teacher in a school that had taken risks for the sake of children, other schools must be doing so as well. I had assumed that teachers would be more sensitive to our human diversity. I had assumed that teachers were current on inclusive terminology. The reality of the situation soon became very clear.

The telephone rang. "Hello. I'm looking for the Indian Consultant."

"Hello, I am the consultant for Indian and Métis Education, how can I help you?"

"No, I wanted the Indian consultant."

"I am the consultant for Indian and Métis Education, how can I help you today?"

"Oh. Well I'm doing my Indian unit and I'd like someone to come in and make bannock or do something."

"Bannock or something" – so my term as educational consultant began. I was soon receiving numerous calls to fulfill wishes to "do something" – "do beadwork"…"do teepees"…"do dream-catchers" …"do stories." At supper one night, I asked my husband, "How do I begin to explain and teach teachers that 'doing bannock' is not enough, that inclusive education should be much more?" In the beginning of my consultancy I was also unable to name or label the experiences that I was having. I had few words that I could use to describe to teachers the inadequacies of their intentions. In my teacher preparation program, which was for Indian teachers, I received minimal instruction on multicultural education. As a teacher, I had chosen to take part in survival basics for my professional development. While I had a sense of things feeling wrong, I was ill-equipped to label the inequities that existed in our teaching practices.

At least there were those who wanted assistance: many teachers communicated that since they did not teach Aboriginal children they had no need for resource materials about Aboriginal people. I felt that so much more could be done in the area of Indian and Métis education, but the challenge was how to warm people to the idea. So I did agree to "do beadwork" and "do stories." However, it was always important for me not to trivialize what it was I was doing. I would begin with a story as an instructional approach to teaching lessons on constellations. A beadwork lesson would include instruction on geometric concepts as well as symbolism in design and color. A lesson on birch bark biting would present information on symmetry. By modelling for teachers what Indian and Métis education could be about they were inspired to participate in it more fully. I also had to clearly state that schools in the future would be made of large numbers of Aboriginal children; however, this was a difficult argument to defend, since I had no concrete data to support this argument at the time.

In my first year I was able to visit every one of our 50 schools. I provided a wide array of services, including providing information on a variety of topics: terminology; treaties; contemporary issues such as land claims; values; racism, stereotyping and discrimination, and racial issues. I provided hands-on learning opportunities for teachers and students through instruction on traditional crafts and traditional games. Usually the choice of instructional methods was through storytelling and demonstration. The storytelling became a commonly requested program. I used the stories as a hook to inspire teachers to become more actively involved in providing integrated instruction; however, in the end I came to understand that teachers really were using the stories as a means to simply entertain students. Many teachers did not prepare for or follow-up on the storytelling sessions. I was very uncomfortable if the request trivialized the original intent of the traditional stories. My struggle was to maintain the intent and the value of the story while not appearing to preach a particular spiritual or religious theory. This would have been inappropriate to all parties: the Aboriginal community for it was not my place to provide spiritual instruction, and the community at large and our system, where we try to maintain religious neutrality.

Personally, I wasn't very satisfied with the approach of "doing" for people. I realized that the approach I had started with was fine in the beginning because it served its purpose: teachers were becoming inspired to find out more about Indian and Métis culture. They began to feel comfortable enough to make requests for more resource materials for use with their students; they wanted to teach in an appropriate way for the benefit of all students. On the other hand, I began to feel like some teachers perceived the role of the consultant as "Let the Indian do it." If I provided the instruction on Aboriginal education then they were excused from having to do it themselves. If I did it they could shirk the responsibility for inclusive practices onto me. It was also easier for them, I think, to call on me: I had access to the materials, lessons and strategies, and in some instances teachers were free to take a planning time, or to make phone calls instead of being present in the class. Some teachers began to grow outright dependent on me to "do it for them." They would attempt to bring me in year after year to do the same thing.

Upon reflection I can see how it was necessary for me to have taken the role of modelling in that first year. Yet it also created some negative dependencies on the part of some teachers. To alleviate the conflict, I sought out the counsel of different elders as well as the consultants in similar positions elsewhere in the province for direction on what I could be doing differently. I read the latest multicultural and Aboriginal research searching for guidance. I took time for reflection. I walked in the evening and sorted out all the information, and slowly a vision for what things should look like formed. I was satisfied with the vision that formed.

> *Coyote saw the lights turn out in the house that sat there on the edge of town. She sniffed the air, twitched her ears and crouched. Cautiously, she ventured into the shadows of the buildings. Stopping here to smell, there to mark her territory. She turned into an alley and disappeared into the caragana. About the time she had reached the park, a new scent was in the trees; she crouched again, eyes sharp, a grimace on her lips. She leaped up, circled once and then again, her tail wagging, quietly she yipped. She was not the only coyote in this village tonight.*

I was pregnant. Year two of my consultancy found me beginning the year with a baby due in six weeks. I made arrangements to attend staff meetings to provide information on how to acquire resource materials, and had the resources delivered to the schools. I presented information on racial sensitivity using a video called *For Angela*, produced by the National Film Board and through the use of reflection, simulation and talking circles. For many teachers and administrators the video and talking circle activities were very moving experiences. As a result of parental complaints in the area of racial incidents, we began to address system-wide procedures for dealing with this problem.

I presented information on the fine line between culturally sensitive activities and those activities that would promote biased views about Indian and Métis people. This was a tough topic to discuss because there are many gray areas when you can cross the line. For example, a teachers' guide based on seasonal themes published by an international company suggested that the teacher should have the children make "potato head Indians" at Thanksgiving, with war paint and a feather and braids. These types of resource materials suggest inappropriate activities that stereotype and trivialize. Examining our teacher resources and being aware and sensitive to the "line" was important for many of the participants in these discussions. I was also learning the lingo; I gained confidence in my ability to "name the issues." I felt I gained credibility when I could specifically label the inequities of resource materials and practices.

Collaborative planning seemed to be a necessary offer to make. I met with two teachers who requested unit-planning assistance. They were not afraid or embarrassed to acknowledge that they really did not understand what integration could be, but wanted to be cautious and appropriate in their choices. I was pleased that they had asked.

I took four months' leave to parent my children, a newborn, a two-year-old and a ten-year-old. Upon my return, I again focused on modeling for teachers how integrated instruction could be done. I placed an emphasis at this time on providing teachers with information and modeling of instructional strategies. This was an essential move in that, while it was a positive step to improve on what we taught, it was also essential to change how we taught to increase the success rates of all children. Talking circles, guided visualization and visual clues to be used in instruction were modelled in classrooms, in-services and staff meetings.

Aboriginal teachers in the system offered their support for future staff development initiatives. The Indian and Métis Education Committee planned a workshop to teach teachers how to make dream-catchers and how to do feather dressing. Leadership amongst our Aboriginal teachers began to blossom. Non-Aboriginal teachers were inspired by the hands-on workshops; there were calls for more. Non-Aboriginal teachers began to identify their responsibility for integrated activities in their classrooms.

A new phase began: I moved from modeling to mentoring. I was happy at this stage to assist teachers in planning, and evaluating their lessons. These teachers began to take a more active role in evaluating resource materials for school purchase as well as evaluating the new purchases made by our system. They began to deliver some of the professional development and they, too, became models to inspire others to also make integrated instruction work.

Mentoring involved some observation around instruction of the content. On only a few occasions were teachers welcoming of me to provide an informal observation of how they had done in their instruction. The mentoring component was most welcome by Aboriginal teachers, and those who taught large numbers of Aboriginal students, in particular in certain programs such as Native Studies.

Mentoring also required that some foundations be created system wide. Teachers had identified the need for subject specific resource materials. While our system already had Myth and Legend kits available, they were constantly in demand and badly in need of repair. An additional kit was created and distributed. As well, several kits were created based on themes identified in our new English Language Arts curriculum. Heroes, Humans and Animals, Me, and a Grade 4 kit on Aboriginal peoples in Canada were created and made available for distribution. At the secondary level, kits on Myths and Legends, an Aboriginal literature kit, and an Aboriginal resource kit were created and distributed through the Indian and Métis Education resource room.

It was in year two that we also began to create a mechanism for evaluation of our progress in the area of education equity. At that point we had been collecting yearly data on the kinds of initiatives undertaken, however our system identified a need for data on our progress in the areas of education equity. Education equity is a program governed by our Saskatchewan Human Rights Commission. It calls for school divisions to report on five key areas:

• Parental Involvement

• Policies and Procedures

• Curriculum

• Recruiting and Retaining teachers of Aboriginal Ancestry

• Cross-cultural training

To facilitate a closer examination of our progress, the consultant who came to replace me while I was on leave prepared a data collection format. It was up to me to begin this process the following year.

> *Folks in town began to talk about that coyote that was hanging around. She was making folks change the way things were done. They had to lock up the hen house and tie up the dogs at night now. They never had to do that before.*

In the first half of year three, I could now see the results of modeling and mentoring. There was a growing confidence in integrating Aboriginal content; teachers were phoning to let me know of resource materials that they thought were biased. They felt comfortable about calling with their success stories and with sharing stories about the lessons that turned out wrong.

I began to work closely with system consultants to challenge them to model integrated lessons in their professional development offerings. The message that was being sent was that integration of Indian and Métis content was the responsibility of us all. I sensed that a foundation was being laid.

I also began to work closely with a woman from our Curriculum Materials Centre that distributes thematic kits system-wide. She was concerned that Indian and Métis content was still being presented in an isolated fashion; her dream was to have multicultural perspectives in all thematic kits. We began by identifying the most popular kits and finding materials by Aboriginal writers or presenting Aboriginal perspectives and we included these materials in the kits. Teachers were then provided with kits that were already integrated – no extra work for them. I jokingly called these initiatives "all part of the infiltration" – but this sounded as if Aboriginal people did not belong in the system. I now refer to it as "permeating the system," because Aboriginal perspectives do belong; this is our system and we value the opportunity to do our share to make it better.

The Indian and Métis Education Committee recommended that a database of resource people should be made available to all staff. In our system we had an on-line computer network that allowed us to look for resource materials system-wide. The aim of the Indian and Métis Resource Database was to empower teachers to find their own resource people from around Saskatoon without depending for information on the consultant. Teachers would then feel that the information was accessible and the hope was that they would then feel better equipped to integrate it.

Aboriginal teachers began to ask for an opportunity to network. The Stirling McDowell Foundation grants afforded us the luxury of funds to cover substitute wages. We were able to free some of our teachers to meet with two University of Saskatchewan professors in talking circle and reflection on the topic of teaching in multicultural classrooms. Many of the participants reflect on how this experience opened up a world of opportunities for them; some are interested in graduate studies so they can continue this process that was begun.

Aboriginal teachers also began to share valuable information about their heritage, traditional knowledge, teaching strategies and resources as well as providing emotional and spiritual support to their colleagues. An education equity forum and feast unified the Aboriginal teachers to allow us to communicate our individual visions. A clearer picture of what we were involved in began to form.

A problem surfaced, however: some folks really liked me to model for them. Some took it as an opportunity to catch up on their marking, change their bulletin boards or bring in a couple of classes so that the teachers were free to collaborate. I realized that "doing" for people had created in some people a dependency. I regretted that they were receiving the message that the best people to "do" Indian and Métis education were Indian and Métis people.

I remember a conversation that I had with a grade 5 teacher:

"Hello Shauneen, Could you come and do that great lesson on stereo-typing that you've done for the past two years for me?"

"Well, Mary* I have modelled that lesson for you twice and I did leave a copy of the lesson plan for you the last time I taught it. At this point, I will have to say that I won't do it for you, but if I can support you in any way I would be glad to."

"Hmm. But, I really liked how you did it."

"Yes, I understand that."

"Well, I guess I'll ask Susan* [an Aboriginal teacher in her school] to do it then."

I spoke with another consultant later that day, I shared my story about dependency. Her response was, "You teach lessons for them!" She commented that as a classroom teacher she felt inadequate to teach math, for example, yet it never occurred to her, nor was it encouraged, that she should ask the math consultant to come to her class to teach those lessons, simply because she did not feel she was very good in that area. That type of information was acquired though in-service and professional development. Good points, I thought. They also solidified for me my vision of the consultant's role.

Another issue that surfaced was the perception of Aboriginal undergraduate students in education. Many of these university students spoke of the unwelcoming environment of the school board office. They told of stories of sisters, brothers and spouses applying for jobs in my system and being treated rudely in the application process. Aboriginal people in the Aboriginal Teacher Education Programs felt that our system did not hire Aboriginal people. We needed to address this misconception. I offered a couple of open-house type of tours for students in the two programs. I also offered to meet with them before they picked up their applications. The numbers of complaints about rude reception were reduced when I acted as a buffer between the applicant and the systems rules and protocols.

That third year was also a time for controversial issues. Discussions began with staff, community and administration around one of our high schools' stereotypical logo, the "Redmen," a name had been quietly talked about for years in our community. I was invited to enter into an extensive period of research to find out why it was offensive and then a plan had to be created for how I could assist in communicating this information to the staff, students and community. The process was well worth the effort, and all parties grew from the experience of presenting opposing views: debate in structured controversial activities, reflection and finally a vote.

It was essential to maintain a high degree of visibility at all levels: in the classroom, with interagency partnerships throughout the city and with my colleagues at the board office. At this point in my term my vision for the system was much more focused and for the first time I was able to confidently communicate what the intent was.

Coyote lounges in the park under a shady tree. She licks her paws and recognizes the children who feed her their crusts from peanut butter sandwiches. She smiles, eyes twinkling. The townsfolk have accepted her, this stranger who moved into town. They tell tales of her curious way of walking straight down mainstreet: head held high, that crooked smile upon her lips. They question what new things she'll try today.

Year four focused on issues of communication. A series of openhouse informational sessions were offered to parents as a result of a growing need to communicate with parents of Aboriginal children. Copies of our education equity reports were sent to all major Indian and Métis governing bodies. The Federation of Saskatchewan Indian Nations, the local tribal council and Métis locals were invited to ask questions about the report's initiatives. I let our inner city principals know that I welcomed an opportunity to meet with parents in their communities to discuss Indian and Métis education initiatives. A parents' open house was sponsored. I was invited to meet with small groups of parents in their homes, at the school and one-on-one.

With this increase in visibility with parents, some began to phone me directly when they had issues that concerned them. I needed to ensure that, while I was a supportive ear, they really needed to address their concerns first to the teacher and the administration at the school.

I was invited to meet in informal talking circles with female students at one of our collegiates. We talked about the issues that were relevant to them. I became an auntie to them; I listened as they spoke. We worked our way through the minefield of issues that they were experiencing: drug use, suicide, sexual abuse and racism. I was frustrated that someone could not have facilitated these interactions in-house, or in the community. At one point, the girls began to bring their older sisters and friends to meet with me. I felt the need to distance myself from the girls, since my ability to counsel was limited.

I worked directly with several Aboriginal and non-Aboriginal troubled youth who needed to know what resources existed in our community and who assisted as work education students. I hope the benefits to them were great; I too, gained from that experience by giving back to my community. One young man finished high school – the first in his family. He won several awards and with the assistance and support of the staff at his school applied and was accepted to an American art school.

Research and information processing was extremely crucial at this point. I began to seek out any quality information that would be beneficial for teachers, administrators or parents. Verna Kirkness' articles from *Windspeaker* magazine in the education section became informational packages to be distributed to all administrators. Short articles on Indian and Métis history, stories and contemporary issues found their way to each school's representative for Indian and Métis education. Community sporting, cultural and spiritual events were constantly being recommended for distribution. I felt an increased sense of urgency as my term drew to a close to keep the focus on permeating the system. The time was ripe for preparing our staff for the predicted changes in our demographics.

Negotiation of partnerships was also a strong focus, for with the ever-increasing student population it was essential to have established partnerships with First Nations and Métis organizations. It was hoped that eventually these negotiations would solidify into partnership arrangements for program development collaboration, and for the sharing of resource personnel. These initiatives were as a result of provincial grants that were made available annually that required a partnership with Aboriginal organizations.

Teachers of Aboriginal ancestry were encouraged to form informal support networks. They were able to achieve this through collaborative research, participation in our annual forum and feast, and with the opportunity to become mentors for others through a sort of

Big Sister/Brother arrangement with new teachers. When last we met, there were plans for "book clubs" to investigate the latest in research in the area of Indian and Métis education.

The focus on modeling remained strong. However, it was also necessary to wean. Materials were provided to schools so that they could begin to help themselves and take on some of the responsibility for inclusive education. Invitations to come to do storytelling were turned down, since this had been modelled thoroughly. Teachers were referred to additional resource materials and names of other resource people were made available to provide a story-telling session. There was much disappointment and in some cases frustration that I would not do it for them. The feedback I was receiving was that teachers wanted me to come and "do" for them. I had to be adamant that the responsibility for integration and inclusive education is the responsibility of us all.

At the end of my term, I left confident that the contributions that I had made were based on solid understanding of my role to inspire, mentor, wean and empower. I am thankful for the opportunity to make to make a small contribution to my system. I am thankful for the growth and understandings that I received.

Coyote left. Folks haven't seen her around lately. They sit sometimes on their front steps and remember. They speak of the funny smile she had and that curious way she had of making them change their old ways and how, well how it wasn't so bad after all to have a coyote in town.

Coyote drinks from the river, looks left and than right. She yawns and scratches her ear with her elegant paw. She sniffs the airs, spots a butterfly. She jumps at it, than sets off with a yip and a backwards glance.

Section Three

Rebuilding Culture: Teacher Education with Urban Aboriginal Peoples

Chapter 8

To Teach from the Soul

*Bente Huntley, Cree-Métis from the Muskoday
First Nations, Saskatchewan, Canada*

*The battle over the future of the Earth is taking place on two fronts.
One front exists in the areas where air, water, soil, and other living
things are being degraded by pollution, clear-cut logging, mega-dams,
development, and so on. In response, environmental groups are
sprouting up all over as citizens battle over issues affecting their personal lives and neighborhoods:*

*The other front is in the minds of people. The real cause of our destruc-
tive ways lies in the ingrained value and belief systems that shape our
outlook and actions. The big question is: how can we bring the perception of all people into alignment with the real things that keep us
alive and provide a quality of life? [Suzuki, 1994, p. 145]*

The Saskatchewan Urban Native Teacher Education Program
(SUNTEP) is an off-campus university program. SUNTEP was created in 1980 to address the need for Aboriginal teachers in the
province, to improve the success rate of education for Aboriginal
people, to provide teachers who are sensitive to the needs of students of Aboriginal ancestry, and to provide positive role models for
Aboriginal students. SUNTEP is administered through the Gabriel
Dumont Institute (GDI) in co-operation with the Saskatchewan
Department of Education, Training and Employment, the University
of Saskatchewan and the University of Regina. The Gabriel Dumont
Institute is the only Métis post-secondary organization that exists in
Canada. Graduates of the program receive a Bachelor of Education
from either the University of Saskatchewan or the University of
Regina. They are fully accredited and may teach anywhere.

I currently teach the science methods class for the Prince Albert
SUNTEP centre. The journey I embark on with my undergraduate
science students is one of learning for all of us. Saskatchewan's science curriculum stresses the importance of gender equity, cultural
perspectives and the STSE (Science-Technology-Society-Environment) connection. This story focuses on these issues, and on the
methods, strategies and reflections used to teach the elementary science methods class in an urban native teacher education program.

The emphasis on respect for the oral traditions of Aboriginal peoples is evident all over the world. It is essential that we as teachers make science relevant and personal for students, especially in an urban environment where people become disconnected from the natural world. Future educators need to be committed to promoting a passion for reconnecting the students who cross their paths with the natural environment. The journey embarked on by my undergraduate students each spring, is, I believe, a step in the right direction to examining the "real things" in life that are essential for survival. As an Aboriginal woman, I want to help the students I teach to create their own maps: to teach from the soul and to trust their cultural heritage. The journey started with the words of my daughter.

"Science sucks"! It was with a great deal of dismay and astonishment that I read those two little words written in bold letters extending from a concept map on the blackboard. Two little words that conveyed so much meaning. I had almost finished preparation for classes the next day. In my undergraduate science class we would brainstorm ideas on the new science curriculum. My 15-year-old daughter was waiting patiently for me to finish so we could go home for supper. While waiting she had quietly relayed her feelings on what she thought about science. I was at first devastated at the words on the board, because of the interest for science that I possess which I hoped (and assumed) would rub off on my daughter. I was about to erase her words when I realized what a teachable moment this would make for tomorrow's lesson. After all we were going to discuss, quite candidly, the students' experiences and feelings about science. What better way to start? The science curriculum stressed the importance of gender equality and Indian and Métis content. Here was a unique opportunity with which my daughter provided me.

I questioned my daughter about her negative attitudes towards science. I asked her why she felt that science sucks. Her first words were "Just because it does." Upon further questioning a few issues came forth. The issue of gender and science is still very much in focus, and she believed "the boys get to do all the fun stuff." As well, the issue of Aboriginal world view and how different cultures view learning science still needs to be addressed in the classroom. To my daughter, science was the least favorite of all subjects and, interestingly enough, the one she found the most difficult, the most useless. Why? That question promoted a lively discussion the next day. All the students had negative stories about science in elementary and high school. Their experiences were either non-existent (they could not remember) or they were quite negative. In each case, science was taught as if it were separate from nature and totally irrelevant to their lives. Therein lies another issue: the Science-Technology-Society-Environment connection. In this chapter I will discuss gender equality, cultural perspectives and the STSE connection. I will also discuss how the Saskatchewan science curriculum deals with these topics and will offer some concrete examples of how I have started to deal with these issues in the science methods class I recently taught. Finally, and I feel most importantly, I will examine the role of the children in the future of this planet; after all, it is why we are educators, is it not?

Gender Equity

> Over half the world's population has been denied access to the competitive, hierarchical, and patriarchal power structures of government and business. Women have a radically different perspective from men, one that is characterized by caring, nurturing, sharing, and co-operation, the very traits that will be needed to stave off eco-catastrophe. It is not an accident that women are so prominent and disproportionately represented among the leaders and the rank and file of environmental groups around the world. [Suzuki, 1994, p. 191]

It was indeed a pleasure and a unique opportunity to teach the undergraduate science class for the first time to an all-female class. This is not because I find males hard to teach or that I do not want them in my class, but simply because it afforded both the students and me the opportunity to feel equal and be given equal opportunities. I did not have to worry about gender equality. Was I directing most of my questions, tasks and attention to the males (McNeil and Schmitz, 1992, p. 1)? Within an all-female class, the women participated equally with regards to gender. They could also discuss gender issues without apologizing to any male members who might be present. As well, they all had to pull their own weight when we were on our two-day science camp. As McNeil and Schmitz (1992) point out, often without knowing it females rely on males for certain chores or for verification of ideas and concepts.

It was indeed interesting to see the students "come alive." An all-female class also meant I did not have to make special sleeping arrangements for our two-day science camp. The learning environment was ideal. It was a wonderful opportunity "to encourage girls to continue trying rather than doing it for them" (MacNeil and Schmitz, 1992, p. 3). In addition, I wondered what impact I (being female) would have on the students' attitudes towards science, since science has been an area dominated by white, first-world males (McNeil and Schmitz, 1992; Pomeroy, 1994; Rose, 1994; Sjoberg and Imsen, 1988; Suzuki, 1994).

The discussions, questions, concerns and comments arising from the two words *science sucks* carried over the remainder of the classes. Gender equity questions often emerged. Do females have the same opportunities in science as males? Are females viewed as equal partners when it comes to science and technology? Why do females lean towards the more compassionate careers in the field of science and technology, as suggested by studies carried out by Sjoberg & Imsen (1988)? These lively dialogues rekindled memories and stories of some of my own more negative experiences in male-dominated fields.

The first year I began the Renewable Resources Technology program at a technical institute was only the second year female students were enrolled in it. However, I was not aware of this at the time. The reason I applied was because the program fulfilled my passion for nature: for working, discovering and learning outdoors. All the classes (except accounting) sounded different and exciting. However, there were many of my male counterparts who felt the program was not a place for females. It showed in their comments, attitudes and actions. For instance, 70 students graduated after two years. I was one of the five female students out of 70 who continually had to grapple and to come to terms with the white, male-dominated attitudes and jests. (There was a drop-out rate of over 50% for females compared to a 20% male drop-out rate.) Out of those 70 graduates, I was the only Aboriginal person to complete the course that year. But I learned how to cope. More importantly, I realized how difficult it was for females and Aboriginal people to "succeed" in science-related fields: a double-edged sword.

What Does the Science Curriculum Guide Say About Gender Equity?

It is the responsibility of Saskatchewan schools to create an educational environment free of gender bias. This can be facilitated by increased understanding and use of gender-balanced materials and non-sexist teaching strategies. Both girls and boys need encouragement to explore non-traditional as well as traditional options. In order to meet the goal of gender equity in the K-12 system,

Saskatchewan curricula reflect the variety of roles and the wide range of behaviors and attitudes available to all members of society. The new curricula strive to provide gender-balanced content, activities and teaching approaches. However, will that be enough when science is viewed as a "man-made activity" (Sjoberg and Insen, 1988, p. 219) by society and other social institutions? As Sjoberg and Insen point out, as science educators (or teachers) we teach about science content, but we might also subconsciously pass on the status quo in social relationships in regards to science (p. 243). As teachers we may communicate that it is not "feminine" to be in certain fields because it is not a woman's role. Therefore, teachers need to consider whether females are given the same opportunities as males in science classrooms and are asked the same type of questions and are treated with the same expectations. According to my daughter and her attitude towards science, these issues are still not resolved, despite the fact that my daughter was taught from resource texts recommended in the new science curriculum. "The difficulty for science educators is that girls and boys can read the sharply gendered message still being sent from the scientific labor market, including that of science education [and educators] itself" (Rose, 1994, p. 156).

Educators may need more time to adjust to the expectations of recent science curricula and for society to feel the impact of these changes. However, paramount to curricular changes must be attitudinal changes towards science. All the curricular changes will not matter if science educators do not apply them. Perhaps we are becoming too lazy and set in our ways to try new ideas, or we may have lost our passion for curiosity and discovery. Maybe educators (elementary at least) do not have sufficient science backgrounds and they themselves suffer from lack of confidence and a "science sucks" attitude.

Teacher in-service sessions on new science curricula are not enough. However, recent teacher graduates have a definite advantage and understanding of the new curriculum initiatives. If educators (especially females) come out of teacher training with positive attitudes towards teaching science, and teach with curiosity and passion towards "science for all," then maybe they will instil passion in their students. The next generation may then be committed to using science and technology for the benefit of Mother Earth and humankind instead of to the detriment of the planet and ourselves.

It was indeed a relief and a bonus to hear my undergraduate class was "turned on" and passionate about science, at least for a time. But will one experience be enough to sustain them through to their own classroom? For some, perhaps, but for others the "traditional" science they were exposed to in elementary and high schools may be too ingrained. Time will tell.

Aboriginal World Views

A new educational consciousness, an "Ecology of Indigenous Education", must be forged, one that allows Indian people to explore and express their collective heritage in education and to make the contributions to global education that stem from such deep ecological orientations. The exploration of traditional Indian education and its projection into a contemporary context is more than an academic exercise. It illuminates the true nature of the ecological connection of human learning and helps to liberate the experience of being human and being related to the natural world at all its levels. From this perspective, education takes on the quality of a social and political struggle to open the possibilities for a way of education that comes from the very soul of Indian people. [Cajete, 1994, p. 218-19]

I thought about how I might teach my science class so that it reflected Aboriginal world views, since this was an all-Aboriginal class taught by an Aboriginal person. How could I make the cultural border-crossing Aikenhead (1995) identifies easier for my students? Pomeroy (1992) feels it is important and necessary to look at different cultures' views of "science." I decided the best way was to follow the advice of the Elders and teach from nature, not about nature and to begin to create our own maps (Cajete, 1996). *To teach from the soul* meant I must trust my cultural heritage and feelings. So the class started with a two-day science camp at McPhee Lake (located just outside the Prince Albert National Park). Field trips are also recommended in the new science curriculum as a "valuable learning experience" (Cajete, 1996, p. 18). The science camp proved to be just that, although it was much more than a field trip; it was a chance for the students to reconnect with nature.

Two cabins were rented and all activities started from these headquarters. Each day started with stories and activities, such as students imagining themselves to be the shutter and lens of a camera. This activity allowed the students to view the natural world in a totally different way, as a close-up quick shot. This activity was designed to awaken their curiosity. Throughout the day students participated in various games and activities, all tied to science. There were a number of stations set up for the students to explore. Each station represented a different ecosystem: lake, slough, forest, sand dune. At each station the students recorded the temperature of the air, water and soil. They examined the water, soil, sand and air for organisms. The students sampled the water and the beaches for plankton and bottom fauna. Meter plots were measured out, where students had to list and identify the various organisms they discovered. They also had to identify any tracks they noticed and list any signs of human interference. As well, what field trip would be complete without a scavenger hunt? In this particular scavenger hunt, the students examined relationships, succession, changes, signs of the seasons, movements, patterns, coverings, cycles and homes. But at night the magic occurred. The students were required to discover and examine the night life of the natural world. Stations allowed the students to observe what organisms inhabit the forest, beaches, air and water during the nocturnal hours. By eleven in the evening the students were exhausted. This was the ideal time to view the constellations from the beach (or in some cases from the top of picnic tables). Students were then encouraged to sit around the fire and create legends about certain constellations. Throughout the camp experience the students were reminded to "walk softly upon the earth," to never take without giving something in return, to use all their senses and to reconnect and bond with the earth.

However, the highlight of the trip was the Treebeard Trail nature walk guided by an elder. Each student was amazed at the knowledge the elder possessed about the forest, the incredible stories that accompanied the tour and the gentleness and respect of the Elder for the natural world. As Cajete (1994) points out,

> The knowledge of Indigenous people about their environment is a testimonial to the ingenuity, creativity, resourcefulness, and ability of people to learn to teach a harmonious way of existence with Nature. (p. 79)

This is a harmony or balance the world so desperately needs now if we have any hopes for survival. Environmentalists, along with other leading scientists, are starting to heed the voices and warnings from Indigenous peoples the world over. Research and literature is full of prophecies, warnings, lessons and advice of those Indigenous cultures who still possess ties to Mother Earth (Aikenhead, 1994; Cajete, 1994; Corsiglia & Snively, 1995; Deloria, 1991; Ermine, 1995; Johnson, 1992; Suzuki and Knudtson, 1992; Suzuki, 1994;). Now is the time to put that advice into action. How can this be accomplished? In 1991, a statement for "Preserving and

Cherishing the Earth" was signed by "dozens of renowned scientists" from around the world (Suzuki, 1994). It is a start. But more must be done.

Gloria Snively (1995) lists considerations for teaching science to Native students for the benefit of all. One consideration is to recognize Indigenous oral traditions and somehow incorporate or adapt written and spoken language to the students' needs. Children's stories and questions about science are important both to them and the teacher. It is difficult for a teacher to have time during a science class period of 30 minutes a day to listen to even one question or story from each student, let alone discuss or answer them. One method that works (if an educator is willing to put in extra time and effort) is the use of oral science journals. Students respond orally to their science experiences on an audio cassette tape. Each individual has a special tape. It is a good idea to provide a recorder in a quiet room or area just in case some do not have access to a tape recorder at home. The oral journals contain the students' experiences thus far. For example, when I was teaching the science methods class, I gave the students a number of questions about their previous "science" experiences in elementary and high school, and among community and family. Both positive and negative stories were accepted. As well, reflections and suggestions were requested about their experiences and activities at the science camp. They were also asked to read an article and respond to it orally. Finally, they were to give an oral philosophy of science education based on their own experiences and reflections. These tapes were handed in to me. Students were asked not to write out their answers since this defeated the purpose of oral reflection. Because a minimum time of ten minutes was set and no maximum (this was a mistake!), the tapes varied from 15 minutes to over an hour. Of course, listening and responding to the tapes required hours of time on my part, and the criteria for marking oral work differ vastly from those applied to written assignments.

However, the use of oral journals not only gives all students, including adults, a unique opportunity to voice their stories, experiences, concerns and questions, but also provides the teacher with a wonderful opportunity to discuss issues that are relevant to each student on a one-to-one basis. Every student in the classroom has the same chance. The teacher responds orally on tape and hands the tape back to the student. It can be an ongoing dialogue or a once-a-year activity. It is a very valuable and valued experience. I have learned so much from my students this way, and I have also rekindled so many of my own memories and stories about my science experiences.

Positive experiences that stand out in my mind about my own science education are the field trips to the school grounds to explore nature. I will never forget examining so many different insects, flowers and trees. I could relate those experiences to stories I learned from my parents, grandparents and great-grandfather, and I continue a love of plants that follows me today. Sometimes it just takes one or two wonderful experiences to keep the passion alive. As educators, that is something to believe in.

However, as stated earlier, the criteria for grading must be different. For elementary grades, the oral journals can be simply an assessment tool to find out where the students are, or it can be used as an evaluation tool. The criteria depend on the purpose and the teacher. I used the oral tapes as a mid-term exam because of the shortage of class time and to promote the oral tradition of Aboriginal peoples.

The increasing return to the oral traditions of Aboriginal peoples is evident all over the world. Oral journals are one way to promote these oral traditions. This strategy teaches children how to listen and then to reflect on what they hear, think and feel. Many Aboriginal students do not speak out often in class, if at all – but they will if given the time and patience. Once Aboriginal peoples were known as great orators.

What Does the Saskatchewan Science Curriculum Say About Aboriginal World Views?

Teachers must use a variety of teaching strategies in order to build upon the knowledge, cultures, and learning styles, and strengths which Indian and Métis students possess. All curricula need responsive adaptations in order to be implemented effectively. (p. 12)

Oral journals can be one of the key tools to use in a resource-based learning classroom to meet the needs of not only Aboriginal students, but all those with differing needs. Oral journals fulfill the integration of language arts, social studies and the Common Essential Learnings of communication, personal social values and skills, independent learning, creative and critical thinking, and technological literacy. The new science curriculum also stresses the

importance of a variety of assessment tools, including oral participation. What better way than through the use of oral journals?
Written journals have long been highlighted as a recommended tool
for assessment in most subject areas, including science (Gallas, 1994,
p. 75). They are extremely useful. But children need to be taught to
listen, to speak up about their experiences and views, and to ask
their burning questions, which may often be overlooked due to lack
of time or shyness. Oral journals have endless possibilities.

When the oral journals were presented as a method of assessment in my science class, they were met with apprehension at first.
However, the students soon realized the potential for use in their
own classrooms. They responded on tape quite enthusiastically and
I enjoyed listening, reflecting and responding to them. The topics
and issues unearthed were varied and relevant. As a matter of fact,
the students surprised themselves in the amount and content of
what they remembered. As well, while talking, other memories and
stories came forth. All they had was a rough outline, and their burning stories and questions led to other stories and experiences. The
oral journals were like a pebble, which creates ripples when thrown
into a pool of water (Borgerson, 1994).

The new science curriculum goes beyond the personal to emphasize what it calls a science-technology-society-environment (STSE)
connection.

The STSE Connection

Someone lost the plan for the brotherhood of man
   and no one's trying to find it anymore.
There's a cold and empty sky where the wild birds used to fly
   And I've never tasted bitter rain before.
And will the grass be gone from underneath the sky?
   Will the golden flowers wither soon and die?
Will the fires burn out the land?
   Will the sea fill up with sand?
   Will the last word ever spoken be why?
Will the last word ever spoken be why, why, why?
   Will the last word ever spoken be WHY?
   - Roger Whittaker (n.d.)

Unless humankind ceases the devastation it has heaped upon Mother Earth, "why?" might indeed be the last question posed. Cries from Indigenous elders around the world echo Roger Whittaker's concerns. Ruby Dunstan from the Lytton Indian Band spoke eloquently and urgently at the "Cry of the Earth" conference held at the United Nations headquarters in New York city, November 22, 1993.

> *I feel pain and anger that in your rush toward development, the fabric of this globe has been rent, and what you call the biosphere, or ecosphere – but which my people more simply call Mother – has been so neglected and hurt. Our Elders tell us we have to do more than save what is left of our traditional homelands. We need to contribute to an overall change of mind...so that human-kind can begin to initiate strategies which will preserve and sustain the environment that all cultures and nations share. (McFadden, 1994, p. 12)*

We cannot bury our heads in the sand any longer. Because of the disconnected views of many peoples, the Earth and humanity are in serious trouble. The signs are all around. Why can we not see? No longer can the consequences of scientific and technological "advances" be dissected from environmental and social responsibilities. Educators need to be concerned and aware themselves.

What Does the Curriculum Guide Say About STSE Education?

> *Actively participating in K-12 Science will enable a student to....understand and appreciate the joint enterprises of science and technology and the interrelationships of these to each other in the context of society and the environment....develop a unique view of technology, society and the environment as a result of science education, and continue to extend this interest and attitude throughout life.*

The STSE connection is one of the seven dimensions of scientific literacy the Saskatchewan science curriculum recommends for the development of a scientifically literate person. This is a commitment and understanding that continues throughout life, and one in which some of my science students recently embarked (others were already committed).

I believe one of the key factors of STSE education is for people (including scientists) to understand that science and technology do not have all the answers, nor can they solve all the problems. The Aboriginal world view does not assume that all the answers are known or can be discovered. Aboriginal people with a traditional world view have a holistic view of the universe. Everything is interconnected, dynamic, ever-changing and mysterious. Nature is not viewed as a natural resource to be reduced and fragmented for exploitation and human consumption, but as a precious gift to be respected (Johnson, 1992; Pomeroy, 1992). Humankind cannot, and should not, know all the mysteries of life. "How arrogant is the human species. Do we truly believe that we must label and make lists of our limited, human understanding of Creations in order to claim the knowledge of the profound simplicity of truth?" (Samms, 1994, p. 56). Western science has somehow laid claim to this "truth" while disclaiming other cultural perspectives on the mysteries of life.

The interconnectedness to all living things (which include rocks, soil, air, water) is paramount. It is a connection striven for with the STSE education. Will it be met? There is hope in the increasing number of "Green Schools" found all across Canada. The push for scientific literacy has opened the doors for environmental education in schools. The results are beginning to show. However, at the risk of sounding too pessimistic, unless major corporations and industries get behind the environmental bandwagon, the destruction of the planet will slow down little. For example, there are major industries that produce their own resource units and kits about the value of forests and "sustainable development" (the very phrase is an oxymoron). These kits follow the curriculum guides, and most of the resources are free, making them accessible to and desirable for educators. How can an industry promote the wise use of forests at the same time as it exploits the forests for capital gains? In using these resources, what message are we sending our students?

As well, even before the implementation of the new science curriculum, companies developed new science texts that followed the core units in the new science guides. Many schools now possess these new texts, which are a vast improvement over the old ones, but teachers tend to use them in the same old way: "Read chapter three and answer the questions that follow." This is not very relevant or exciting for students.

Another push in the new curriculum is resource-based learning. This does not mean teaching straight from one text, no matter how "teacher-proof" the texts are. An example of resource-based learning is the use of the recommended books such as *Keepers of Life* (Caduto and Bruchac, 1994). Caduto and Bruchac present wonderful teachings from an Aboriginal perspective about the interconnectedness of life and our responsibilities as members of the two-legged family to "all our relations." Another rich resource is Project Wild, a series of workshops presented by the Canadian Wildlife Federation. The workshop manuals are full of activities centred around conservation, environment and responsible actions.

The last day of my undergraduate science class ended with a full-day workshop from Project Wild. As a culminating activity, the students participated in a role-play. Each student played a different role about an environmental issue (in this case, whether or not to build a dam). The students had a lively town-hall discussion and examined concerns, issues and questions raised from a variety of viewpoints. They debated the issue through many pairs of eyes. Role-play is a little-used, but effective tool that I hope the students will carry with them to their future classrooms. It is also recommended as a teaching strategy in the Saskatchewan science curriculum.

Role of Children

> Those with the most at stake in decisions being made now by governments and in boardrooms of business are youth. After all, they are the inheritors of what will be left. Consequently, they cannot afford to wait until they reach the age to vote....the sense of power and optimism that youth can change the world are contagious, and young people will be a formidable force. Not only are they informing politicians and business leaders that they want change, but they are recruiting their peers and exerting influence on their parents, too.
>
> Youth cannot be ignored. (Suzuki, 1994, p. 191)

Youth are powerful advocates and have the most at stake for the future. For the sake of the survival of Mother Earth, these voices cannot be ignored. But just what can children do? How can we turn the attitude around that "science sucks" to one of concern and commitment to "walk softly on the Earth Mother's breast" (Summer Rain, 1985, p. 63).

Numerous youth organizations now exist in Canada and around the world. For example, the TREE (Teenagers' Response to Endangered Ecosystems) Club is a grassroots organization established to help save South Moresby. As well, in 1989 the EYA (Environmental Youth Alliance) was established by Jeff Gibbs. Gibbs was a 22-year-old University of British Columbia student when he established the group, but the main impetus behind the organization now are mostly females (Suzuki, 1994, p. 216). Another example is Suzuki's 12-year-old daughter, Severn, who started ECO (Environmental Children's Organization) in 1990 (Suzuki, 1994, p. 22).

It should not take a child to tell us to change our ways and to remind us we have responsibilities, not only to them but to the Earth as well. As Suzuki states, "We know with absolute certainty that our children will inherent a world with radically diminished biological diversity and extensive global pollution of air, water, and soil. If we do love our children, what excuse can we possibly have for not pulling out all stops to try to ensure that things don't get worse?" (p. 225). Severn Suzuki presented a plea to the Earth Summit Conference at Rio Centro, Brazil on June 11, 1992 (part of which appears at the end of this chapter). If a small group of 12- and 13-year-olds can raise enough money to attend a conference because they are "fighting for [their] future," we should not look for an excuse for ignoring the problem of environmental degradation.

At the heart of the Saskatchewan science curriculum is the concept of scientific literacy for all, through a resource-based, relevant, student-centred approach to learning science. The curriculum guide provides a variety of ways scientific literacy can be accomplished. It also stresses the importance of gender equity and Indian and Métis content. But educators' attitude and understandings must also change.

Children come to school with a natural curiosity about the world in which they live. We must not, as educators, destroy that curiosity instead of igniting and nurturing it. From an early age, children's (especially girls') attitudes towards science changes drastically from one of interest and curiosity to the idea that "science sucks" (Sjoberg and Imsen, 1988). The target age appears to be the early teens, but I feel children need to be encouraged and nurtured from day one. A negative attitude towards anything is not fostered overnight. Unfortunately, poor science teaching starts early and can build each year. The content of science and other subjects is not the only spiralling influence over the years. Although the science curriculum is resource-based and exciting, science teachers still just assign readings and questions. The new science text series recommended by Saskatchewan Education are very exciting and full of ideas, follow-ups, experiments and activities. From my observations and experiences as a mother and an educator, I believe that some teachers who use these texts do not follow any of the suggestions. Most schools have offered in-service workshops to introduce the new curriculum.

It will then be a challenge to educators to incorporate these strategies and philosophies to teach from the soul. Science will never become relevant and exciting for children if we cannot bring ourselves to find the relevance and passion.

Can humanity be saved? In the critical stages of Mother Earth's cycle, has humanity, through technological breakthroughs, exceeded the limits of her tolerance and healing powers? As Cajete (1994) says, "If our collective future is to be harmonious and whole, or if we are even to have a viable future to pass on to our children's children, it is imperative that we actively envision and implement new ways of educating for ecological thinking and sustainability" (p. 23). New ways or new "maps" should include Aboriginal world views and women's perspectives. Suzuki talks about the new leaders as "the third world, women, youth, elders, and Indigenous people" (p. 190). Today, those voices are crying out not only to be heard, but to be heeded as well. For the sake of the survival of Mother Earth and humanity we must listen. The journey on which some of my undergraduate students embarked, is, I hope, a step in the right direction to examining the "real things" in life which are essential and important for survival. We must listen closely and take up the challenge of our youth and elders.

I'm only a child yet I know if all the money spent on war was spent on ending poverty and finding environmental answers, what a wonderful place this Earth would be.

At school, even in kindergarten, you teach us how to behave in the world.

You teach us:

*not to fight with others;

*to work things out;

*to respect others;

*to clean up our mess;

*not to hurt other creatures;

*to share, not be greedy.

Then why do you go out and do the things you tell us not to do?

Do not forget why you are attending these conferences, who you are doing this for – we are your own children.

You are deciding what kind of world we will grow up in.

Parents should be able to comfort their children by saying "Everything's going to be all right. We're doing the best we can. It's not the end of the world."

But I don't think you can say that anymore.

Are we even on your list of priorities?

My dad always says, "You are what you do, not what you say."

Well, what you do makes me cry at night.

You grown-ups say you love us. I challenge you, please, make your actions reflect your words. Thank you for listening.

(Severn Suzuki in Suzuki, 1994, p. 229-230)

I still have hope for humanity, and for my daughter.

References

Aikenhead, Glen S. 1994. "Towards a First Nations Cross-Cultural Science and Technology Curriculum for Economic Development, Environmental Responsibility, and Cultural Survival." Presented at the International Organization for Science and Technology Education, Alberta, Canada, August 1996.

Aikenhead, Glen S. 1995. "Toward a Cross-Cultural Perspective on Western Students Learning Western Science: Border Crossings." Presented at the National Association for Research in Science Teaching, St. Louis, Missouri.

Borgerson, Lon. 1993. "Storytelling in Play: Upisasik Theatre Revisited." Master's Thesis. University of Saskatchewan, Saskatoon.

Caduto, Michael, and Bruchac, Joseph. 1994. *Keepers of Life*. Saskatoon, SK: Fifth House Publishers.

Cajete, Gregory. 1994. *Look to the Mountain: An Ecology of Indigenous Education*. Durango, CO: Kivaki Press.

Corsiglia, John, and Snively, Gloria. 1995. "Global Lessons from the Traditional Science of Long-Resident Peoples." In *Thinking Globally about Mathematics and Science Education*, edited by G. Snively and A. MacKinnon. Vancouver, BC: University of British Columbia, Centre for the Study of Curriculum and Instruction.

Deloria, Vine Jr. 1991. "Traditional Technology." In *The Circle Unfolds: Indian Education in Canada*, edited by M. Battiste and J. Barman, pp. 28-32. Vancouver, BC: University of British Columbia Press.

Ermine, Willie. 1995. "Aboriginal Epistemology." In *The Circle Unfolds: First Nations Education in Canada*, edited by M. Battiste and J. Barman, pp. 101-12. Vancouver, BC: University of British Columbia Press.

Gallas, Karen. 1994. *The Languages of Learning*. New York: Teachers College Press.

Johnson, Martha, ed. 1992. *Lore: Capturing Traditional Environmental Knowledge*. Hay River, NWT: Dene Cultural Institute.

MacNeil, Toni, and Schmitz, Jan. 1992. "Teaching Science as if Girls and Women Counted." Presented to "If Women Ran Science" conference, University of Saskatchewan Women's Studies Research Unit.

McFadden, Steven. 1994. *The Little Book of Native American Wisdom*. Rockport, MA: Element, Inc.

Pomeroy, Debra. 1994. "Science Education and Cultural Diversity: Mapping the Field." {unpublished paper? publication details?}

Pomeroy, Debra. 1992. "Science across Cultures: Western and Alaskan Native Sciences." *The History and Philosophy of Science in Science Education 11*: 257-67.

Rose, Hilary. 1994. "The Two-Way Street: Reforming Science Education and Transforming Masculine Science." In *STS Education: International Perspectives on Reform*, edited by Joan Solomon and Glen Aikenhead. New York: Teachers College Press.

Samms, Jamie. 1994. *Earth Medicine*. New York: Harper San Francisco.

Sjoberg, Svein, and Imsen, Gunn. 1988. "Gender and Science Education: I." In *Developments and Dilemmas in Science Education*, edited by Peter Fensham, pp. 218-48. New York: The Falmer Press.

Snively, Gloria. 1995. "Bridging Traditional Science and Western Science in the Multicultural Classroom." In *Thinking Globally about Mathematics and Science Education*, edited by G. Snively and A. MacKinnon. Vancouver, BC: University of British Columbia: Centre for the Study of Curriculum and Instruction.

SummerRain, Mary. 1985. *Spirit Song*. West Chester, PA: Whitford Press.

Suzuki, David. 1994. *Time to Change*. Toronto: Stoddart.

Whittaker, Roger. (n.d.). "Why." *A Special Kind of Man*. RCA records.

Chapter 9
Voices Given to Us: Contextual Theatre in an Urban Native Teacher Education Program

Ron Borgerson et al., Teacher-Director of
SUNTEP-Prince Albert

This is a collective story. It weaves together the response journal entries of students in an urban native teacher education program as they create an original play, perform it and reflect on its significance in their lives....It is a story about voices.

* * *

It seems like we are starting from nothing, but of course that's not true. We are starting from ourselves.

We are students and staff of the Saskatchewan Urban Native Teacher Education Program (SUNTEP-Prince Albert), and we are here to make a play. We are seated in a circle, around a large sheet of paper, brainstorming possible topics and taking turns as recorders. This is a SUNTEP Theatre tradition. This is how we begin.

Kim: Each time we roll out that huge sheet of paper, I feel so intimidated because I know that the only way our idea can be successful is if we all work together as a team and not be afraid to contribute.

Choosing a topic isn't as easy as it seems. There are 24 of us in all, and we are a "new" group, a cross-year group, with a few students from each of the four years of the SUNTEP program, including three who have just returned from successful internships.

Valerie: This is a big group, and there's a lot of energy circulating in the group. I look forward to working with these individuals. I some-

---

*with student-actors Sharon Ashby, Janice DePeel, Tyson Drabinasty, Trish Dyer, Kim Fiddler, Christie Goodfellow, Jason Gyoerick, Kurtis Hamel, Angela Johns, Valerie LeDoux, Lana Lorensen, Karen Moreau, Myla Murray, Linda Netmaker, Dorothy Olson, Laurie Paul, Jodi Pocha, Carla Omani, Heather Scriven, Tracy Sylvestre, Corey Teeter, Dwayne Tournier and Christine Wright

*times take life for granted, but when I was interning I sure missed
SUNTEP. It's a people place, where there's love, hope and understanding.*

*Jodi: I [even] feel insecure with the upper years. I can't imagine how
some of the first years feel. I know that by the end we'll all be comfortable and one large happy family, but how do we get there?*

We come from all over. Some of us are from Cree, Dene or
Dakota First Nations such as Mistawasis, Fond du Lac or Wahpeton,
but most of us are Métis, from the Prince Albert-Duck Lake-St. Louis
area, or from northern communities like Pine House, Meadow Lake
or Ile-a-la-Crosse. (The "Métis" are "mixed blood" people, with a
cultural heritage that is both diverse and distinct. Our history and
ancestry may vary, but we all belong to the "Métis Nation.") As
Métis and First Nations students, we have come to Prince Albert's
SUNTEP centre to earn a bachelor of education degree from the
University of Saskatchewan, and to participate in SUNTEP's mandate: "to ensure that people of Aboriginal ancestry are adequately
represented in urban teaching positions." This is why we are here,
but it is not what truly connects us.

At SUNTEP, we belong to an amazing community of teachers
and teachers-to-be in which we often learn more from each other
than we do from our university courses. We learn from our social
and cultural differences and from what we share in common. We are
Métis and First Nation, rural and urban, young and not-so-young,
but most of us are women, many are single parents and nearly all
have lived below the poverty line before coming to SUNTEP. Issues
of race, class and gender intersect at our centre – we have many stories to tell.

SUNTEP Theatre serves as a venue for our stories. Once a week
we meet to create and perform our plays, always with our own stories as foundation. All of our plays have been collectively created
and performed by students and staff on themes and issues that matter to us. This is "contextual theatre" because our personal, social
and cultural life provides the context for our drama work.

Our first play, "Martha" (1989), was a classic example because it
chronicled the journey of a typical SUNTEP student through our
program.

*Martha: I don't know what your problem is! You should be able to
help me out by doing your share of the housework around here. You
don't have a piano strapped to your ass.*

Spouse: The only piano strapped to my ass is you!

Martha: Just wait...In two more years I'll graduate and you'll be kissing this piano!

With the Oka Crisis in 1990, it was inevitable that our second play speak to the issue of land rights for Aboriginal people. In "The Great Canadian Golf Crisis," Prime Minister Macaroney decides to turn every reserve in the country into a lush green golf course, administered and managed by a newly created Department of Golf Affairs (or "Golf Canada"). His plan backfires. Métis and First Nations people respond by blockading "the whole damn country." ("Nobody gets in and nobody gets out.") They are assisted by Wesakechak, the Cree trickster:

Newscaster: This is a special news bulletin....A most unusual situation has developed across this country. Animals, thousands of animals, are blocking our roads, rivers and airfields. Bear and moose have been sighted, patrolling highways and border crossings. Caribou are reported to be locking horns and closing off airport runways. Rivers have been dammed by beavers. Wolves, deer and elk have been closing off all roads and railways, and flocks of birds have settled over the airports of this nation....Yes folks, those very animals that we see on our stamps and on the backs of our pennies, nickels and quarters have turned on us!

In the end, the Canadian Army surrenders, Macaroney is led away in a straitjacket and Wesakechak invites the audience to live their dreams, their fantasies. "Golf Crisis" was performed at the 1990 World Indigenous People's Education Conference in New Zealand.

In 1992, we created "Wheel of Justice," our irreverent response to the quincentennial celebrations of Mister Columbus' arrival on this continent.

Narrator: And now, ladies and gentlemen, it's WHEEL! OF! JUSTICE!....From our courtroom in downtown (Prince Albert), it's North America's most watched game show! The famous wheel is spinning away, with lots of verdicts and an assortment of fabulous and exciting sentences, from small fines to life imprisonment, just waiting to be won tonight!

Using a game show format, this play takes Christopher Columbus to court, charged with indecent exploration, vending without a license, defacing public property and breaking immigration laws. Nina, Pinta and Santa Maria are his character witnesses:

All Three:...

Take us out on the ocean

Take us all for a ride

Give us some cultures that we can attack

Give us some slaves that we can take back

Cause it's hip, hip, hip for Columbus

If he don't get gold it's a shame

For it's Nina, Pinta, and Santa Maria in the new found land!

The play is all humor and farce until "voices from the past" testify to the 500 years of genocide that Columbus set in motion, and the play ends in a celebration of survival and solidarity. "Wheel of Justice" was published by Coteau Books in an anthology of plays for high school students (Suntep, 1993).

Gambling became a hot issue in 1993, and we explored a variety of perspectives in "Kisiyinew," which means "old man" (or "elder") in Cree.

> *Voice: If we could get into the business end, the working end, instead of the playing end of gambling operations, we could build our own casino-bingo complex and the money would stay in our community. We would attract outside interests: okimawiak, with lots of soonias. Mooniasok, with big pockets full of money and a lot of high hopes. They would play at our casino until their pockets are empty, then they would leave the reservation with nothing...I say we do it! Let's go for it! Let's build the biggest and best casino complex in North America!*

During the performance, we turn the theatre into a casino, with everyone in the audience out of their seats, gambling. Each game presents a different aspect of Aboriginal self-determination (education, justice, economic development), with the odds heavily loaded in favor of the dealer. The games end when the cast is "busted" and taken away by the Prince Albert City Police (a cameo appearance by a local constable). The audience returns to its seats to hear the final words of the "elder" in our play and to consider the issues we have raised.

That same year, we were asked by the Prince Albert Mayor's Committee on Family Violence to create a video drama that might be used for workshop purposes. As we developed scenes for "Silent Voices" (1993), we soon discovered that nearly every one of the women in SUNTEP Theatre had experienced spousal abuse. Our scenes and stories were not invented. They were re-enactments.

We continued to explore gender issues in "Family Feudalism" (1994), which used a game show format to satirize men's attitudes towards women. This was a women's play, with women playing the roles of stereotypical males like Biff Jerky, Harley Davidson, Frank Furt, Axle Grease and Puck Enright. During the "commercials," the contestants slip out of their comic roles and speak candidly from their own experiences with men. With the final question ("How are we going to make things different?"), the game ends in chaos. And then each actor steps forward to speak directly to the audience.

> *Josie: My grandmother worked long hard hours to sustain a family of eleven children. My mother tried to instil those same values in us. It is up to us to teach our children, our sons and daughters, of the hardships that the women of the past have had, so that we can have a brighter future. Yes, it is bread we fight for, but we fight for roses too.*

Our latest production, "A Thousand Supperless Babes" (1996), chronicled and celebrated the story of the Métis. To create this play, we researched Métis history through literature, archival material and, more importantly, the stories and photographs of our own families and communities. A story of the Métis emerged that was authentic and relevant, that celebrated our ancestors: Philoman Allary, Christine Pilon, Judith Parenteau Dumont, Angeline Gouldhawke....all portrayed in role by their descendants in SUN-TEP Theatre.

> *Angeline Gouldhawke: In 1922, the school at Wahpeton opened, and all my children went to school there. On one side of the aisle were the settler's children, and on the other side of the aisle were the native children. They say this was because the native children were funded by Indian Affairs, and the white settlers' children were paid for by the province. I don't know if that's true, but I know this always troubled my husband. His family, his children didn't fit on either side of the aisle. They weren't native; they weren't white settlers....They were Métis.*

"Supperless Babes" resonated with local and provincial audiences, and then with international audiences as well, at the 1996 World Indigenous Peoples' Education Conference in Albuquerque.

In and between major productions, SUNTEP Theatre functions as a theatre-in-education troupe, with numerous performances in local schools. These plays are inspired by stories and legends, by tricksters (*Wesakechak*) and monsters (*Witigo*), and by issues as diverse as "bullying" and "curfews." So, on certain afternoons, we bundle our giant puppets, black lights and other paraphernalia into a convoy of vehicles, and set out to visit another school.

All of these plays, for audiences young, old, near and far, begin in a circle around a large sheet of paper, and that's where we are now, in January 1998, considering topics for SUNTEP Theatre's next collective work. Our web grows: "single parenting," "racism," "drinking and drugs," "high school drop-outs," "peer pressure," "abuse," "suicide"....until the sheet is filled with topics. We want to do them all, every single one, because these are all issues that concern us as educators.

In this first phase of the collective process, there is often a group desire to "do it all," to address all of the issues that we see around us. Narrowing the focus of the play is often tricky. However, given the size of our group, we need one inclusive topic that will draw us all together, and three possibilities finally arise. The first is to create a new play that celebrates SUNTEP.

> Heather: As a fourth year (finally), I would really like to do a play about SUNTEP. It has been my life for four wonderful, stressful years. I am going to really miss SUNTEP, the instructors and my friends.

The second topic is a last-minute entry, and is both whimsical and intriguing: a play about "love." The story possibilities are universal and endless, with all kinds of room for both laughter and tears. The third topic is a play that honors those who have inspired and supported us, a play that celebrates our grandparents and parents. And, when the final vote is taken, this is our choice.

> Kim: I like the idea of family – and honoring our families. With the audience being our families. I am torn between who I would honor – my mom or my dad. I could probably think of a nice story to tell about both. My parents are a big part of my life and contribute a lot to my success. My mom gives me patience and perseverance to stick things out and my dad gives me humor, strength and courage to be who I am.

The next phase of the collective process is pure and simple: research. Each of us must choose someone we wish to honor, and we must begin gathering stories.

> Jodi: When I mentioned this to my grandparents, whom I'd like to honor, they seemed really interested. I have tons of stories; however, I plan on prying out more this weekend. Sundays are always storytelling days.

> Laurie: I can only hope that my grandmother is having a good day when I go to talk to her. I only wish I wrote the stories down on paper

when she and my grandfather would tell them. My grandfather is gone now. Actually, I went over to my mom and dad's yesterday and he said that he could help me.

Kurtis: It's a toss-up between my mother or my great-grandfather whom I don't know, but I do know he fought in the 1885 Rebellion and is in a picture with the captives after the Rebellion.

Heather: My sister and I were left in Prince Albert with my auntie Janet and my grandma on the weekends. I really appreciate what they did for me as I was growing up. These two people played a large role in my life, and I don't think I've expressed my gratitude enough to them, so I would like to honor one or both of them in a story.

Sharon: My problem is that my grandparents have all been gone for over forty years, and only my mother lives. She does not talk about her past; it seems like it was unhappy. I have only recollections of old stories my dad told me...But I would like to emphasize to our audience to treasure all the memories and carry them over the generations. I'm really envious of people (adults) with grandparents today.

Tracy: At home I have this picture frame, but it has no pictures in it. It's one of those multi-picture frames. It sits out, and people ask me, "Trace, how come you have no pictures in it?" And I tell them, "It's for the family that I have not met yet...but one day there will be pictures in it."....When someone comments on how I look, I think and wonder about how my ancestors looked. Who do I look like? It's a curious happy feeling, because I was adopted and I know one day I'll meet them.

When the stories arrive, SUNTEP Theatre becomes a storytelling forum. Theatre is, after all, a form of storytelling. It shares the same elements: voice, movement, sound and silence. It engages an audience, evokes tears and laughter, carries meanings and memories, extends our oral traditions. So, in small groups, we share our family stories, marvel at the connections with our own lives and, as Clarissa Pinkola Estes (1994) observes, find that "The first story almost always evokes another, which summons another, until the answer to the question has become several stories long...."

Sharon:...Each morning, we would find two black things about the size of a pencil eraser hanging on a string to the outside doorknob. Before we went in the house we were told by Grandma to take those black things off the string and eat them. Well, what a treat! They tasted like licorice and I really enjoyed the flavor. We always thought of them as candy. But, years later, we found out those black licorice candies were actually laxatives, and we were always very regular kids.

Laurie:...Dad said it never failed that his grandfather would have to tell a very scary ghost story before bedtime. The children would go to bed and their grandfather would try to scare them. Either scratch on the walls, tap on the windows, or make scary sounds. Dad said it would take forever to go to sleep.

Jason:...When my dad was young, he had a race up a stack of hay bales with one of his brothers. My dad beat my uncle up the bales, so when my uncle started nearing the top, my dad pissed on his head! After hearing that story, my mom bugged my uncle, saying: "That explains how you got your rosy cheeks."

We shift imperceptibly from the research phase into dramatic exploration. Some of our stories are chosen for group improvisations, and eventually make it into our play. Most (like those above) are set aside for another day, another play. In past productions, the story-line has determined the scenes, and somebody has had to assume the role of director, organizing and overseeing the whole affair. This play is different. We are all directors of our own scenes, or vignettes. Each of us must choose the person we will honor, the stories we will tell and how best to dramatically present these stories – through monologue, improvisation, mime, shadow play, puppetry, song, dance, poetry, diary, tableau or by weaving these forms together. We therefore move into the next phase of the collective process, staging and production, with each of us making theatrical choices for our own stories.

Jason: I have really been thinking about my "Vignette" and this is what I've roughed up in my mind: On a blackened stage, a spotlight comes up on me and I say, "My grandparents have always been a very important part of my life..." The light will begin to fade on me as I begin my speech. I will end by saying, "My grandparents are a real inspiration to me and many others whose paths they've crossed, because they've stuck together through the good and the bad and made their love strengthen over their almost sixty four years of marriage together."

Janice: I figure my story is enough. In my family we are strong and stubborn. We tend to wait until it's too late before we express our emotions. So I think the story, told in darkness, with the periodic change of photographs is enough. I don't think it's important for people to see who is telling the story. It's enough that the story is heard. I feel its power and it scares me.

The vignettes are kept fairly private at first, shared only with a few others, in workshop sessions. But time is beginning to press in on us. It is mid-February before we know it and our first perform-ance is on March 17.

> *Lana: We really need to share and show the individual vignettes now. Today, when we were talking about "the play", I thought, "What play?" It's going to take a whole lot more before it can be called " the play." Whatever "the play" turns out to be, I know that it will be awe-some because we have an awesome group of people. If we could just get together more often it would be easier. It seems like we never have enough time. Exactly the message we want to get across: There's never enough time for the important stuff in our lives! Like: Sharing stories, getting to know each other and ourselves better, visiting and laughing with one another, remembering our heritage and sharing it, feeling proud of who we are and expressing our thanks to those we care about.*

We move into rehearsal, arranging and rearranging the order of vignettes in order to create a balance of scenes and monologues, action and stillness, humor and travail. Although we contribute to each others' vignettes, it is only in our first full rehearsal that we finally see all of the vignettes and the play as a whole. We laugh, we cry together, as we show our stories.

> *Janice: Today was very emotional for me but I told my story and that has been a hurdle I have been afraid of jumping for <u>quite</u> a long time. I made it through and I can breathe easier. I have gone over the story in my head a few times and I've repeated it out loud. This has really been helping me.*

> *Valerie: I am so impressed to see how our play is going together. Our rehearsal was very personal and very emotional. I now can see all the vignettes weaving together. I can see the different languages being honored for the audience. This will be a powerful play.*

We decide that Carla's vignette will go last so that she might per-form a Fancy Shawl Dance for all who are being honored in our play. But we struggle with the opening of the play right up to our first per-formance, which we are all a bit nervous about. It is for a local high school, one that has a very low Aboriginal enrolment, and we won-der how these teenagers will respond to a play about "old folks." We need a setting for our play, one that will contextualize our vignettes and illuminate our message. We decide to lead with a scene that highlights the hectic pace of our lives, something with lots of action and noise.

> *Jason: I like the idea about the chaos even before the play starts. I think when it stops though, we should have the entire room black and some-one gives a little introduction: "In our urbanized everyday lives, all of*

the hustle and bustle keeps us from looking at the people who have worked so hard to make this world a better place for us to live in..."

To create "chaos," we experiment with television commercials, but this gets dropped along the way. For teenagers it will be fine, but many of our "family" audience will be elderly and may not appreciate the raucous collage of television commercials that we have in mind. We decide instead to begin with music and dance.

Our centre has a dance troupe, and many of them are in SUNTEP Theatre, so we recruit their services. We begin our play with jigging and pattern dancing, which escalates to country rock ("I'm in a Hurry" by Alabama), with strobes and stage lights pulsing, and the whole cast on stage, gyrating faster and faster as the music builds. Then, in ice storm style, we fake a power failure: the power crashes, the sound dies, the lights black out and the cast is left in confusion. What to do next? How to go on with the show?

With a few technical glitches, this is how our first performance begins, and our teenage audience seems to fall for it. The chaos and commotion seem real. Then someone in the cast brings out candles, and someone else hangs coal oil lamps, and someone recalls the old days, before electricity, when people made their own music and, on evenings like this, told stories. Then, in candle-light and lamp-light, we begin to tell *our* stories.

My great-grandfather played the mouth organ and the violin. His daughters would get up and dance while he played.

I realize today that going to those old-time dances with grandma and grandpa was very special, not only because I was with them but because I believe they danced through me.

The French they learned to speak fits more into the category of the Michif language, and Grandma is the best bannock-maker I know.

Unfortunately for grandpa and myself, our dear little Blacky drank some anti-freeze and died.

February 14, 1886. Dear Diary, We have decided that we are going to get married this summer...Only time will tell what the path holds for us and what the future will bring for us, and for our children and grandchildren.

He was always quite poor and didn't have any horses, so he would ride his bike all the way from Loon Lake to Duck Lake to see my granny.

You see, my grandfather was of mixed heritage. He was both Cherokee and African, and this didn't sit well with my grandmother's parents.

But, like they say, "Love leads the way", so they got married without their permission.

Our family tree reads like a Métis history book, with famous names related to the Resistance of 1885.

My mom doesn't need to speak. When she smiles she lights up the whole room.

But whenever she and the family travelled, she would search through the local phone book, searching for a familiar name. A name to a face she hasn't seen since she was three years old.

(In Cree) Grandmother wasn't watching where she was pointing the needle as she sewed. Grandfather was sitting beside her, also watching "The Three Stooges". Every time she stretched the sinew, she would stab Grandfather in the leg.

I remember kohkom getting very angry with me because she thought I was pretending not to understand her language, which was Cree.

My dad was about three years old at the time and when Grandma served him his meal and he saw the spareribs, he said very excitedly, "Mommy, is this two-bone steak?"

So I walked right over, grabbed her wig, chucked it across the room. And everyone looked at me like, "What is that little kid doing?" But my grandma couldn't do anything but laugh because she hated that wig!

My grandpa's warm heart and comforting manner lives deep within me and I will always remember how much he loved me.

[In song] Always a joke and there to please, friends and family on our knees

We'd forget our troubles, and turn around with a smile.

[In Dene] Today my dad is 68 years old and still traps. Trapping is his life. There is no way he will quit what he loves doing, even though he is getting too old for the bush life.

It must have been hard for my parents to sit by and watch their only girl, their precious girl, doing this to herself. How helpless they must have felt!

Then this frame will be filled with the pictures of the people I haven't met. The ones who have given me my true, self-respecting identity. My black hair, brown eyes, and brown skin.

A lot of people have told me I remind them so much of my grandmother.

Behind us, as a backdrop to our vignettes, photographs appear on a large rear projection screen – photographs of those whom we honor in this play. As Carla dances, a picture of an old man and lit-tle girl (Sharon) is projected behind her. He holds a bouquet of lilacs in one hand, the hand of his grandchild in the other. With this as a final image, the cast forms a semi-circle facing the audience, and Lana speaks the final words of our play.

> As you can see, we have so many stories to share. When we started to make this play, we found out that our whole lives are made of stories. But our lives sometimes get so busy and hectic that we forget about our past, and we leave our elders and ancestors behind. We need to think about where we come from to find out where we are today. This is very important in today's world. So ask your parents and grand-parents about who you are and where you come from. Their stories will enrich you. They will give you knowledge of the past and inspi-ration for the future.

Although the high school performance is by no means perfect, the audience is enthusiastic in its response, and we know we have a play.

> Janice: I tried to change my vignette, but the words were just there, and flowing and spoken before I had time to think and time to stop them…The tempo or beat or whatever just seemed to speed up and the ending is so bitter-sweet. And when I had finished telling my story it felt good. It felt right.

> Sharon: I think it was a great day for us. The whole performance went smoothly. Everyone works together, helps each other, laughs and cries together, and a few of us on my side patted each other on the back. The feeling of closeness has brought us all closer, and we need this close-ness to put our play together.

> Angela: Everyone needs to work at it. The worst was timing! People also need to work at *telling* their stories. I know it's hard not to mem-orize, but we all need to tell it from the heart. However, there was a feeling that it has come a long way. I think that people should practice, practice, practice! And if they are in scenes, maybe rehearse on Monday right after set-up and then in the quick run-through before our "big" performance.

On the following Monday evening, we perform our play for its intended audience: the parents, grandparents, families and friends of the actors of SUNTEP Theatre. The performance is open to the public, of course, and draws many who are familiar with our work, but it is a SUNTEP evening, of poignant moments, of tears balanced with laughter. For some of those honored, the dedications are a com-plete surprise.

Kurtis: My Mom said that when I did my monologue, Lorna [a friend] grabbed her hands and said "Oh Claire" and they both started crying together.

Heather: My grandma cried and she thanked me over and over again, The next morning she called and thanked me again. She told me that we are an inspiration in their lives as well. I thought that was very special.

Trish: Our audience listened very carefully and heard all the emotion, whether joy or pain, that was put into each vignette. The audience absorbed that emotion, laughing when we laughed and crying when we cried. As I heard someone say, at the end of our performance, "Why aren't they handing out Kleenex?" I know in my heart that everyone in the audience was touched in some way that night.

Kim: The performance felt so right. Everything seemed to click perfectly. The audience truly appreciated it. The ending was especially beautiful when we went and handed roses to people in the audience.

Angela: It felt fabulous. For me it nearly mirrored that feeling I had when I heard "Kia Ora" throughout the crowd in Albuquerque. Indescribable really, Just a wonderful warm feeling. Proud.

By this time, two additional performances have been booked. The very next day, we pack up our gear, and move our production to Mont St. Joseph's Nursing Home. As we are setting up, our elderly audience arrives, most of them in wheelchairs. Only after we go into the audience at the end do we have a true sense of how well we have done.

Jodi: After our performance for our families, I had a really difficult time getting "up" for the Mont St. Joseph performance. In fact, that day I slept in. I dreaded the idea of performing. Yet, when they started wheeling in the residents I knew why we were there, and I was "up" to performing. We had a definite purpose and they loved it!

Valerie: Our show at Mont St. Joseph was the highlight of my drama experience. I observed the audience while we were doing our play. Some were attentive, some were in a world of their own. Others looked lonely, some were at peace with themselves, and some took a nap. I sang my song for those elders, and I was happy to do that, to show them that at SUNTEP they are not forgotten.

There is a serendipitous side to the collective process. Something always happens that pulls everything together. It may not be predictable, but it is somehow inevitable.

When SUNTEP Theatre searched for a way to connect "The Great Canadian Golf Crisis" to Maori audiences in New Zealand, we discovered that the Métis and the Maori had both been subjected to the same imperialist emissary, General Frederick Dobson Middleton. We therefore had Macaroney call on Middleton for help. In "Kisiyinew," we discovered that "casino" sounds like "kisiyinew," which means "old man" in Cree. In "Wheel of Justice," someone suggested that we use a wheel of fortune to determine Columbus' guilt. And, in "A Thousand Supperless Babes," we discovered a narrator, Honore Jaxon, whose incredible life led us to begin our story of the Métis in, of all places, New York City.

This year's serendipity is the sudden scheduling of a provincial Métis Elders' Conference in Prince Albert and, with one week's notice, an invitation for SUNTEP Theatre to perform. The conference just happens to fall during the performance week of our play, so it is a perfect finale. Two days after the Mont St. Joseph performance, we present our play for the last time, at the hotel where the conference is being held, and the audience is the most responsive we have had.

> *Kim: The last performance at the Métis Elders Conference was awesome! The elders were really into the play. I looked out to the front row and there was an elderly man with tears in his eyes - that was when I realized just how powerful our voices really are.*

> *Jason: I feel they got hooked into the play because it revived many memories, and many people knew at least one person being honored. I met some relatives for the first time...When Grandma and Grandpa's wedding picture turned up. I heard some voices gasp and say "Oh look!" So then I knew someone had recognized them.*

> *Sharon: I feel it was the icing on the cake. So many of the people gave us hugs, and one lady would not let go of my hand. I think we did ourselves proud.*

> *Janice: One elder told me that "You can see it in her eyes," referring to my mother. "I hope one day you find her. The girl with the picture frame too. Our table, everyone sitting around here, cried. We have been here. Our people have been here and so we feel for them. We lost our parents when we went to the residential schools. All the young people should see your play so they can see how much they have. These stories are important. They can learn from them. They need to know this and so I thank you for what you have done tonight."*

After the performance, we pack our gear for the final time, load it into trucks, then cluster together in front of the hotel. There is lots of laughter, lots of racket, many hugs. A police car cruises by, checking us out. No one wants to leave.

It all begins around a blank sheet of paper; it all begins from "nothing." And when it's over, it's time to look back. What meanings does this kind of theatre have in our lives as individuals, and as students and teachers in this urban native teacher education program called SUNTEP?

Just before the first of our performances, we circled up to choose a name for our play. We brainstormed and discussed a long list of titles and eventually settled on this: "The Voices Given to Us." It is true to the spirit of our play; it speaks of the strength that everyone draws from those who have gone before. But as we reflect back on the collective process, the title of our play takes on other meanings. It speaks of the personal, social, cultural and professional meanings that the play held for us. The voices given to us.

> *Corey: SUNTEP Theatre, in a way, is therapeutic; it gives the students the opportunity to discuss difficult and/or personal issues in an environment that feels safe and open.*

> *Trish: We went back to our family members and searched for stories that would make us understand ourselves. Some of us found stories that would make our lives more complete and make us understand ourselves better. Others found barely anything because all of their stories were hidden, or had passed away with their loved ones. I believe in my heart we made "The Voices Given to Us" because we are all searching and yearning to find and understand ourselves.*

> *Myla: We learnt about ourselves. When we returned and shared our research or stories within small groups, we learned about others in the group. It seemed everyone was developing a sense of pride from their stories. Our confidence was raised after seeing similarities and a common bond in each others' stories.*

> *Carla: We all have to share our stories to carry on who and what we are, where we come from and where we are going. We can't be selfish, because we may never get past ourselves and we will not teach others. Our stories, no matter how simple, always have a meaning. This is why it is important to listen to others when they are talking and telling their stories. We may not use them right away and we might not even remember them, but stories told and listened to will eventually help another person out.*

> *Lana: The stories were not made up, or fictional, they were real and very emotional. In sharing these stories with others, we allowed ourselves to open up, and, in some cases, this is the first step towards healing…We will always remember this play and how it touched our lives. This is because the material was so deeply rooted in our personal lives.*

For many, our play was a personal journey because it gave voice to personal and familial stories. This was both therapeutic and empowering, but there were social transformations as well. We found voice as a group, as a collective. We changed a lot from the early sessions when we didn't really know each other all that well.

> *Angela: We were all so different, all from different years of the program, different personalities, different ages, and different walks of life. It was strange. And then we started working on our collective. We laughed together, cried together and groaned together. We were becoming a group.*

> *Christine: I learned qualities such as patience, understanding, compassion, persistence and respect. As part of a group, I also acquired some new learnings. I know how to be a team member, take responsibility, participate, contribute, trust. I know the importance of friendships and relationships and, most of all, to have fun!*

> *Tracy: To look internally and receive a person's story without judgement is part of the collective learning experience. Can we carry away a new perspective about someone from an already conceived notion? Yes, and this is a learning experience. I did not only learn about myself in my part of the play, but, as well, I believe my part allowed people to learn things about me they had never known.*

> *Trish: We have reached into our hearts, deep down into them, and pulled out the issues that have meaning, not only meaning, but profound meaning. Issues that brought laughter, silence and tears to our eyes. Issues that brought us closer together, as if we had known each other all our lives, yet some of us just met.*

> *Angela: I see a group of people that I have come to admire. A group of people that are still as diverse as when we first met, but now we have a special bond. We have the bond of stories. I will cherish the memories we have made, the stories we have told and the experiences we have shared. I have learned a lot from this group. I think we have now given voices to each other!*

And to each other's cultures as well. "The Voices Given To Us" reflected the cultural diversity of SUNTEP and the sense of family and solidarity that we hope will someday be mirrored in the world outside our centre.

> *Kim: In such a fast-paced world, who would ever think of making a play honouring our grandparents? That's not profitable! No, it may not make any money or be a big screen hit, but I tell you it has a far greater effect, because it brings hope to people that maybe life isn't about fancy clothes or big cars. Maybe, just maybe, it's about caring, loving and being a part of a family, where you are safe. A family can*

be anywhere – at work, home or school. Anyplace where you are encouraged and supported. SUNTEP Theatre is this to me and to many many others who have either participated or been in the audience at a production.

Heather: *"The Voices Given To Us" didn't only bring meaning to our audience but to our drama group itself. I was given the opportunity to take time out and listen to my grandmother's stories, something I would not have done otherwise. My grandmother and I had a wonderful discussion and she made me laugh and cry. She shared a great deal with me. I also discovered many old photo albums that she had tucked away. Some of the photos were from the early 1900s. It was great.*

Jodi: *During the creation of my own vignette I opened a "storage room" full of stories in the minds of both my grandma and grandpa. Since our play Grandma has "opened up" and shared with me many more stories, many of which I wish she would have shared with me earlier. My cousins, who saw the play, realize how much knowledge and stories Grandma and Grandpa have to share with their grandchildren. They are starting to ask questions like never before. It is great! I'm not the only "nosy" one anymore!*

Linda: *From start to finish, "Voices" had a purpose, an understanding, a taste that you can feel in your mouth, a meaning for the people that we were honouring. What I learned from this play is how very important my heritage is, my culture is, and to be proud of who I am.*

Corey: *In our play, we also used other languages [first language], traditions and customs [Carla's dance]. Our play was extremely diverse and didn't entirely focus on one community or culture.*

Christie: *Our play expressed our identity as Aboriginal people and as growing individuals. The energy we created through the play will last for a long time.*

Lana: *In our stories, you could see the evidence of poverty, racism, prejudice, and other forms of oppression. Through telling our stories, we gained hope and inspiration for our futures and for our children, grandchildren and great grandchildren. For to truly see the future, we have to look at the past.*

Karen: *"The Voices Given To Us" reminds me of when I would go and stay overnight at my uncle's. He, too, had fifteen kids. We would set a large circle of stones and make a fire in the centre, and we would tell stories till three or four o'clock in the morning.*

Toss a stone, a pebble, into any pool of water and it will create ripples. We have all experienced the collective process and know the power that contextual theatre can have for its participants. And we know that we can create the same magic in our classrooms. We each hold this pebble in our hands, this experience in our hearts, and we know the personal, social and cultural meanings that we can make with our future students.

> *Janice: One day I will have a classroom. We will clear a large, open space on the floor. In the centre will be a blank sheet of white paper with some markers beside it. My kids will brainstorm issues that have meaning to them. From this they will select a few topics. One will stand out from the rest and this will become the theme of a new play, a new pebble. In this group, as the play forms and takes shape, a ripple effect will begin. The children will research and gather stories, asking the questions that need to be asked. A reflective journal will guide them along the way. After incorporating the stories or message of the play with music and dance and visual arts, they will have learned to trust and support each other. The pebble will be complete and whole, ready to drop into another pool of water.*

References

Estes, Clarissa Pinkola. 1993. *The Gift of Story*. New York: Ballantine Books.

SUNTEP Theatre. 1996. "A Thousand Supperless Babes." Manuscript.

SUNTEP Theatre. 1993. "Wheel of Justice." In *Eureka: Seven One-Act Plays for Secondary Schools*, edited by J. Lewis and D. Warren. Regina: Coteau Books.

Section Four
Touching Earth
in the City

Chapter 10
Stories of the People: Success in Urban Settings. the Inner Strength of "Indianness"

Dottie Kingman, Westminster College, Fulton, MO; Bill Walters, Lakota; Sharon Wells, Choctaw

This chapter focuses on the experiences of first-, second- and third-generation Natives living in urban centres. A thread of narrative runs throughout this chapter, since stories are important to people, dealing as they do with the basic needs of life. The chapter explores how urban Native people use stories, and how they interpret them without the immediate context of the land. For many, the land is the teacher, and humans and other animals are the students. Human beings are the caretakers of the earth, which nourishes all beings. The chapter describes how urban Native peoples deal with the issue of learning from the land among the crush of so many people, and how they find their understandings of the great life-force, the mystical ways of communicating with Mother Earth and other people. The values of urban Aboriginal people about privacy will also be examined. How do urban dwellers cope with daily repeated invasions of the self? The writers will share urban Aboriginal people's thoughts and values about how to sustain themselves in their exile from the land in the face of daily incursions of the mechanical life of the city.

A characteristic frequently stated about modern life in the United States is that people are mobile. They do not stay where they were born or grew up. Therefore, few people have access to extended families. In general, it is becoming increasingly rare to find adults living where they were born or grew up and rare to find them living among families and communities who have done the same. American Indians are the exception to this fact of contemporary U.S. life.

Those Indians who are currently living in urban areas may see themselves as part of their own people, even though they are not physically living in their own nations and reservations. This ability to remain part of a people and to have a "homeland" or home place seems to underlie the success some Indians have with urban living.

We interviewed and talked with 30 adults: members of the Oglala, Navajo, Akmiel O'othem, Cheyenne River Lakota, Cheyenne, Crow, Standing Rock Sioux, Oklahoma Choctaw and Oklahoma Cherokee peoples. All of these adults are college-educated professionals and are involved in Indian Education. Some are teachers and administrators working in schools; others are part of the larger educational organizations that support the federal government's treaty obligations to provide education to American Indian children.

All of those we talked with grew up on or adjacent to their home reservations where their parents and grandparents spent their lives. However, instead of staying on their reservations, these individuals have lived their adult lives in metropolitan areas. With few exceptions, they plan to return to the reservations to live. As a group, they did not express the alienation from their culture that one might expect. In part, this seemed to be due to the jobs they held. Their financial status allows them to return to their homes at least once a year and for special events, and, because they work in organizations set up to deal with the education of Indian people, they are around other Indian people and their practices and concerns.

While many in the group were aware of Indian centres and services in their locales, few took an active part in such structures. They felt that the time and finances the centres and services have are better spent on Indian people who do not have as many resources. They occasionally participate in special celebrations and programs, but do not take day-to-day advantage of the services and tend to find socialization among colleagues from work and other organizations.

We were interested in how they maintained their "Indianness" in the press of urban settings, in how and whether they educated their children in Indian ways, and in how they felt their lives would be different if they resided on their home reservations.

The following questions seemed particularly important to the interviewees:

• Do you feel a spiritual attraction to the earth? Is there a particular location which most attracts you?

• Tell us the stories of your people.

• In what ceremonies or celebrations do you participate?

- What difference in your life has living in the city made? How do you think you would be different if you had lived on your reservation/land?

- Someone has said that Indians can only reside in cities, they can never live there. Do you ever feel in danger of losing your "Indianness"? How do you maintain it?

- Tell us about your Indian language.

The people combined these questions to tell stories of their lives. The short excerpts that follow are representative of the stories we heard.

* * *

[From a person who lived 19 years on the reservation and has been in urban areas for over 25 years.]

I feel a spiritual attraction to my home and to the buttes. There is a sense of calm and quiet that comes over me. Part of it is memories of growing up there, but there is a larger power. I have learned a lot living in a city. I have access to more things. I don't have to drive ninety miles to get something. I have grown used to the comfort of urban living. On the reservation the people's view is more limited in some ways. Many are dealing with poverty so severe that outside events do not matter to them. It is a poverty that few in the city can imagine. I think the despair may be the same, but urban poverty is not like reservation poverty. I know many Indian people who have truly lived in cities. They find ways to get their Indian needs met and they find a sense of community. But they do not understand the land the way a person living on the reservation would. I know who I am. I always know I can trace my relatives back to 1850 and that they were here long before that. My children, too, know who they are, even though they have not grown up on the reservation among the people. But they do not have the closeness to people or land that I had, growing up on the reservation. I keep in contact with relatives back home, calling and writing a lot. We prepare corn soup and other traditional foods. We participate in local Indian activities. I never spoke very much of my language, but I do understand a lot of it. Since I do not hear it regularly, I am forgetting how to understand much of it. I know traditional stories of my people and teach these to my children. I grew up near where the Ghost Dance occurred and that hope and power is part of me. I don't want to grow old in the city. Someday I will return to my reservation.

[From one who lived his first 16 years on his reservation and has lived in urban settings for over 35 years.]

My parents and grandparents lived on the reservation. I will return there. I know the stories of my people and teach them to my children. The stories always have a moral and a message and are used to teach children discipline, that is respect, for their lives and others' lives. Indian people do not use stories like the boogie man to teach right ways of acting. I know how to use the winter count to diagram history. I know the story of the sacred pipe and how it was brought to my people. I know the stories of skirmishes between my people and white settlers. I know the story of the massacre at Wounded Knee. I feel a spirituality at Wounded Knee. I regularly participate in purification in the sweat lodge and in prayer and healing ceremonies. One should not take such things lightly. I was raised Catholic, and I worship God, who is found in everything. I have talked with medicine men and we have explained things to one another. Living in the cities has allowed me to get higher education. I have been exposed to other cultures and nationalities, other people. This has helped me appreciate differences and to understand others. But the cost is high. I sometimes know I am losing touch with "the people" and the longer I am away, the more loss. My home is Pine Ridge; I reside in West Virginia. I think people of all races can understand the land by living on it and caring for it. I know what I am, where I came from. In my heart I am a Sioux. I talk to people about my tribe and other tribes. We Sioux get together and socialize. I always know that if all else fails or all else succeeds, I have some place to go back to. By choice I will go back to my land and people.

[From an individual who lived on the reservation 12 years and in urban areas over 45 years.]

My parents lived off-reservation for thirty years and I am generally not informed about the stories of my people. These stories have become important to me in later years and the people who could teach me are all dead. I didn't want to know the stories when I was young. I wanted a successful way of life, a life that was successful by other people's standards. I have a sweat lodge in my backyard, but it is from Scandinavia. I think I am fully integrated into life here in the city. I have become very non-Indian. If I had stayed on the reservation, I would be a lot more prejudiced and intolerant and provincial. People on the reservation are so isolated. Indian children feel alone and unwelcome when they go away to school. I think I've lost my Indianness. I have discouraged the Indianness in my children; they will work in a non-Indian community. I return every year to check on my property and to visit relatives. I have a homestead for retirement.

My feeling is that preservation of Indianness is a worthwhile endeavour. As I am older, I feel this way – I didn't when I was young.

[From one who lived on the reservation for 22 years and in urban settings for 28.]

I will return to the reservation when I retire. It is my home. I miss my language. I know a lot of the stories of my people. My relatives always brought in older clan people and fed them and they told stories. I tell the stories to my children. My family goes out to Crow to participate in ceremonies. I sing Crow songs here. My children dance and sing and speak a little Crow. The Crow way is that human beings are caretakers of the earth. I think it is all Indians' way. I feel a spiritual attraction to the earth on the reservation, not necessarily here in the city. I believe we are all tied to "He who makes all." Even though I live in the city, I am Crow. I socialize with Indian people and I work among Indians. My family has maintained our Indian culture. We sing Indian songs, speak Crow, pray in Crow at night and most of our friends are Indian.

[From a man who lived on the reservation for 20 years and in urban settings for 25.]

I will return to my reservation because it is my home, the place of my people. I know many stories of my people and how they came to be. The stories help me know that nature is important in my life and I teach the stories to my children. My children are also involved in ceremonies and traditions like the sweat lodge, the naming ceremonies. They have been to the Sun Dance. Such things are very important to our lifestyle and how we interact with other people. Mother Earth is our survival. Any place near home has a spiritual attraction for me. There is a power all around us. I do not feel that I am losing my Indianness, but my children and grandchildren do not have the closeness with the land because they are not there. Living in an urban setting adds to this. If I had stayed on the reservation, I would not have seen that parts of it were ugliness. I would have been a substance abuser. In the city, I burn sage and sweet grass. I study and read about my Indianness. I use my higher off-reservation education to help me better understand my reservation and my people. With this learning I have to talk with people and get learning of the heart also. I only learned to speak my language later in life when I learned it from an elder.

[From a woman who lived on the reservation 19 years and in urban settings over 30 years.]

Most of my sisters still live on the reservation in the Low Mountain area where we grew up. I have a hogan there and go back often. One of my uneducated sisters takes care of my sheep and animals. I'll live there all the time some day, because my relatives are there and the things I grew up with, the mesas, the plants, the sheep, the people. I know many stories of my people. Some I learned growing up; others I have learned in college and through study. My children know these stories and keep in close contact with their relatives. They spend the summers with my sisters and our elders. My daughters have all had Kiinalda. We have ceremonies regularly to keep in balance. We go to dances and ceremonies. We feel close to the land. I think all Indians do, though we can really mess it up by white man's standards, I mean with trash and junked cars. I feel at peace with the Creator when I am up on the mesas. When I'm at home I get up before sunrise. Living in the city has let me get formally educated, meet other people and find out how the rest of the world works. I would not send my children or grandchildren to school on the reservation. I want them to have opportunities that they wouldn't on the reservation. I want them to be able to function in the urban world, but to also appreciate their Navajo roots. I am not sure any of them will want to live on the reservation, but they sure do want others to, so they can visit and be part of activities. I think all people want to be where they grew up and to remember only good things about it. That's why my children don't feel the same way I do about the land. They were born in cities and grew up there. But I think they are still Indian and know there are certain ways to treat people. They have respect and obligations to certain people, to their family. We travel to the reservation at least monthly so I think we are in contact. My children might be more at home in the city than I am. I know I am just visiting here and really live among my people and the mesas and the land.

[From a man who lived on the reservation until age 20 and has been off-reservation in an urban setting for 12 years.]

I notice many differences between being on the reservation at home and living in the city. This is a western city, so there are not many tall buildings and it isn't really far to "wide-open" spaces. But it is still different than the reservation. Everything here seems to just rest on Mother Earth, to be temporary and ill at ease. Nothing seems to be a part of Earth, like the hogans at home or the pueblo buildings. There is lots of landscaping here. There are beautiful plants, but they all seem to be artificially placed, too contrived. At home, every inch of ground has some kind of life on it. You might look out and think it's barren, but when you really look, and the most elderly tell us to look, you can see so much life, plant and animal, everywhere. I was anxious to leave the reservation. I wanted to see things and do things. Even the most remote rez place seems to have a television dish. Maybe television is the great cultural leveller. Like Anglo young people, I wanted to break away. I love my family and my people and I dreamed of doing things which would help them. I thought I could do them better off reservation. But I notice that when there is any crisis in my life, a stress, even just a thundershower, I am essentially Indian. I revert right back to my prayers and ceremonies and ways of dealing with such events. I can feel all my put-on city Anglo ways dissolve instantly and I am reaching in my mind for a Navajo way to solve things. This is a comfort to me as I get older. I return to the reservation often, so that is how I stay Indian. I think it is possible to be an Indian in the city. I know who I am. There is no doubt I'll end up right back on my family's land in a few years. I like the comforts and availability of everything here, but it doesn't really talk to anything that I really am.

These excerpts and short descriptions are typical. Yet they belie the complexity of the lives of each of the tellers. Life on many reservations is hard by any standard. Yet these hardships are often not told or emphasized. The learning that people received, the grounding they feel, is what they chose to tell. The group of people we talked with seem to credit their early experiences with shaping their daily lives and their idea of what their future will be – a return to their homes.

There is one story in particular that we have received permission to retell in longer form. It seems to personify the importance and essential nature of being Indian. We feel this person expresses what growing up on the reservation did for him. Growing up on the reservation seems to have been a partial source of his self-destruction, but at the same time was his salvation. Here is the story in the words of a Lakota who lived 23 years on the reservation and as many years off, who lost his way and almost his life, but who remembered how to find life again.

I was born on the Indian Reservation a few years back. I came from a very poor home, but I did not know that. In fact, I just really enjoyed life when I was young because I had a very loving family. I used to love to play in the creeks and rivers near my home and on my grandparents' ranch. In the winter, my big brother used to tell me stories. When we'd wake up in the early morning and I would look out the windows that did not have boards on them, the windows would be full of frost from the cold nights. We would be wrapped up in thick blankets and look at the windows and I would hear the story of "Jack Frost" as told by my brother. My brother was always full of all kind of stories.

I had a tremendous love for animals and my brothers and I would go to our grandparents' house with our father and we would ride horses and play in the barns. My grandmother was always telling us about the importance of animals and she spoke in our native language so my brothers and I were able to learn how to speak the language as well. My grandmother would take us on long walks and tell us about plants and roots and how important they were. She told us that people should take care of them and use them for food and medicine. Grandma would grow huge gardens with lots of good things to eat.

My father was rarely at home when I was little because he was trained as a heavy equipment operator in the army and there was no demand for heavy equipment operators on the reservation. My father was a warrior, having served his country in World War II, and when he was home we had some exciting times. He would take us on walks to the river and tell us about cars and trucks and work on the big dams he was building. He always made sure we went to grandma's house.

On the eve of my fifth birthday, an event took place that was to change my life forever. I had spent the day with my brother and father, and we had gone to a city away from the reservation. My father had purchased toys and clothing for us and we had fun driving across bridges and then back to Grandma's house for the evening. That evening before going home, my father had noticed that his car was not operating properly so he asked our uncle to take my brother and me home. This was the last time I saw my father alive because early in the morning of my birthday, my grandfather arrived and told my mother that he had found my dad on the road in his wrecked car and he was dead. As the years passed, I was told that dad's death was related to alcohol consumption.

I spent a lot of time with my animal friends after my father's death and, as often as I could, I would spend time with my grandmother. She somehow knew how to ease some of the pain. She helped bring the joy back into life. At the age of seven, my mother remarried and this was the start of a long and ugly emotionally abusive relationship with my stepfather that continues today. I longed for summers to come and school to be out because it was at that time that I could return to the ranch and live with my grandparents and be away from the abusive relationship. Grandma continued to love and nourish my being and she taught me so many things. We would go and pick berries or we would take her 410 gun and shoot prairie chickens for dinner. Grandma taught me how to say thank you and how to give back to Mother Earth for those things She provided for us. My To Ka Shila or grandfather taught me to give and take from the earth only that which I needed and to never destroy things just for fun. My summers were very special as I was growing up. Life on the ranch was hard. My brother and I worked very hard. But we longed for the ranch when we were in school and while we were caught in the abusive relationship with our stepfather.

When I was in seventh grade, I lost my grandmother to diabetes. This was probably one of the saddest times in my life because I lost such an amazing teacher, friend, and grandma.

With this loss I started on a different mission, and that was to work to get away from the abusive relationship in my life. My focus became to get what I could out of life. I started to strive for the almighty dollar. I left the reservation and the ways I had learned from my grandparents. Without those strong ties to my culture, I was left to fend for myself. I was not happy, and I saw many members of my family die. In one thirteen-month period, eleven family members died. Nine of these deaths were drug or alcohol related. Ugly things continued to plague my life. I had successes by white man's standards. I was making lots of money; I had a big house. I was successful in business. But to me, my successes were short-lived because I had little substance in my life. In my late thirties I saw that I was going in the same direction as many of my family members. I realized how sick some of my relationships had become, especially with my wife. I had become a mental and emotional abuser. I had gotten all those dollars and things I had striven for, but none of that really mattered any more because I had wandered so far from the early teachings of my grandparents.

It seemed that each direction I turned there again was despair. I wanted something different. I was at a meeting in Denver and I was inquiring of one of my friends how to get a pipe to pray with. I knew that this was one of the things that I would need to start with. Actually I asked him where I could buy one and he just laughed at me and said that I would not have to buy one. So I asked how do you get one, and he said you have to ask a medicine man and gave me the name and address of a man that I could write to. So the next week I wrote to the man and just forgot about it because I thought I would never hear from him anyway. At about this time, a friend asked me to participate in a "sweat." I told him that I would go and see what it was like, but I was worried that something would go wrong. I went to the sweat on a Thursday evening, and it was one of the most powerful experiences I have ever had in my life. My body was totally drained, but I felt clean and there was a good feeling in me. There was such a bonding between the individuals in the sweat, and I did not even know most of them. I was able to focus myself. On the Saturday following the sweat, I received a package in the mail and it was the pipe wrapped in sage and a letter from the elder telling me what to do. I had a feeling it was a sign that I should start making some preparations.

It was not very long after this that things started to totally fall apart in my life. There were times when I went into deep depression and the thought of suicide was ever-present. I knew that I was not going to last. During the next two years all the aspects of my life started to change and I was torn between two worlds: one of money and greed and living high; the other one of using the traditional ways and staying at the drum, doing the sweats and talking circles. Many times I was totally confused because I was not sure what I even wanted.

Many times I would sit and just cry because I felt I had no guidance and no direction to go. The confusion I felt during these times was ever-present, and even when it appeared that I was adjusting well and all was going well, I still felt I did not know what direction to turn. I was always reversing myself and starting to go back into the state of depression or at least the state of denial. Denial of myself as a person, as an Indian. I had come to believe that Indianness was not a good part of my life and that it was something that I should place behind me. Usually that was because the people I was trying to communicate with did not understand that part of my life either. So who was I to get guidance from? I couldn't get it from those I considered my friends. It was a case of "If you can't like [sic] them, join them." It was also easier to do. It was at these times that I was experiencing a false sense of security and it was so good and so easy to live in that denial. The constant nagging of my spirit continued, and I would slip back into the world of alcohol and substance relief. I was the abuser I had so hated among my people and had tried to get away from.

I finally just moved away from my family. In the next few months I left my job of twenty years and sold my home of fifteen years. In the split I sold all the things I thought were of value and paid off debts and just gave a lot away. I was so desperate to get away from what I believed were the problems in my life. I moved into a small apartment and spent the next eight months of my life in what I refer to as a healing period in my life. During this time I went to the drum and started singing and drumming with my brothers and sisters from my tribe and others. I started forming bonds and finding out about the various ceremonies and how to heal myself or at least ask the Creator for guidance in my journey back to "the People." I attended traditional sweats and warrior circles and I started seeing I was not alone in my quest to heal. Many of my brothers and sisters have fallen from the Good Red Road and are striving to get back. I would sit for hours with the pipe and ask the Creator to give me the guidance that I so needed to go on with my life.

I tell you this story for several reasons. You see, I believe the Creator has always been with me and that he has protected me through those times in my life when I neglected to take care of myself and was so careless that I could very well have not been here today. Many of these events have lead to my vision for education today. I wish to bring traditional culture back into the lives of young Indian people. The real successes I have achieved in my life have been directly attributable to the traditions and teachings that I was taught so many years ago by my father, grandmother, and grandfather, and when they were gone, the teachings continued through other members of my family and extended family. I have come to love and respect all of my Indian brothers and sisters no matter what tribe. The cultures are rich with good things and good thoughts about life and the Creator and Mother Earth. Some of the stories of the people are so fascinating and when the elders speak to the little ones, you can see the lights come on in their young eyes. It is indeed these teachings that will once again bring the people together. Together in peace and harmony as one with the Mother Earth. This balance is what is needed to bring the people back to the ways of the Creator and to have the eagle scream once again with pride.

The man who tells the above story is nationally recognized for making a difference in the lives of the children and community where he works as an educational leader. He talks of the importance of his Indianness, of how he lost it in an urban setting, trying to become something he found he didn't want to be.

The people who kindly spoke to us and shared their lives expressed gratitude for the things they learned and were learning because they were Indian. They spoke of the importance of being connected to the land, their relatives and people, and of the importance of always knowing they have a place to call "home" and of knowing that is where they will return.

Closing Reflections

Rita Bouvier and Angela Ward,
Saskatchewan, Canada

These closing reflections are conversational. The first pages of this chapter are written stories of our lives, cultural and educational, which we offer so that readers understand the perspectives we bring, as editors, to this work. From these short life-writings evolved a conversation, which began with reading each other's stories and developed into a broad discussion of the educational issues stimulated by our book. The themes foreshadowed in the Introduction are revisited here from a more specifically educational perspective, with the intention of supporting teachers in their work of care and advocacy for Aboriginal students in urban settings.

Life-writings

Rita: I was born into the world speaking Michif, a language whose foundation is Cree. *"Kipaha la porte"* (close the door) is an example. I was raised in Iles Bouleau or Birch Island, situated in Sakitawak or Ile-a-la-Crosse. My first teachers were my mother's parents, my aunts and my uncles.

Like many who lived in northern Saskatchewan, our primary livelihood was fishing, hunting, trapping and gathering what nature provided. This was supplemented with food we grew in our own gardens. If *Kisimanitou* (meaning "kind creator") had created paradise, this was it.

I left paradise at age thirteen, and will always remember the day the yellow bus came to take me away. My late grandfather, who had primary responsibility for raising me, had come to understand and accept that our way of life was changing, and so encouraged me to continue with my schooling. I understood early the risks involved; and I came to understand the significance of what he said to me on that day I boarded the bus that took me and many of my friends away from our community to Prince Albert, Saskatchewan. *"Nàtanis, ahpô etoki kawanikiskisin hahkiyaw kîkway ka kikiskinohmâtak, ahpô etoki kawanikiskisin kiwahkohmaganuk, ekwa mina ahpô etoki kamistahitimi-son.*" ("My daughter, perhaps you will forget everything we have taught you, perhaps you will forget your relatives and perhaps you will think you are better than us.") His caution was based on experience of what happened to people who had left the community. Some of them never returned. Some came back, but pretended they could not understand the language any more when they returned to visit, and some upon their return home acted as if they knew better than those who remained in the community.

Growing up in Ile-a-la-Crosse, with its rich history and its connection to Louis Riel, the Catholic missions and the fur trading companies that monopolized this part of the country contributed to my own identity. One did not grow up in Ile-a-la-Crosse with an identity crisis. Stories reinforcing who we were as people were in abundance in the community. I was fortunate to be born there, to have the benefit of a solid foundation, a history and a cocoon-like environment within my family, where individual character was honored and respected. For example, everyone was given a nickname. Nicknames often carried a story to sustain individuals and to show they are loved for their unique being.

Then I arrived in Prince Albert to attend high school. Many of my classmates did not survive this ordeal. I made it, but only with tremendous support from my family, in particular an uncle who would not accept my overture to quit school at one point. In Prince Albert, I understood for the first time what it was like to live in a racially framed world. Not many of my teachers in Ile-a-la-Crosse believed I would make it, except perhaps Mr. Walz and Sister Beaudoin. My family believed in me, and I believed in myself. Away from home, at thirteen years old, I felt a deep sense of loneliness and longing (a feeling I am unable to shake), and so my education has not been without a price.

During this time I learned to deal with the racism around me. I learned that ignoring the ignorant behavior of individuals was best. Addressing this issue required self-discipline, awareness and most of all respect, respect for others and respect for oneself. The temptation to reduce your own behavior to the same ugliness that spews from some people's hearts and mind is always there. I am *eskew* (a woman), and that word embodies the dignity I hold as a human being.

My decision to attend the University of Saskatchewan and pursue a career in teaching was my own choice. Because of financial constraints, I attended university full-time and worked part-time.

My career in teaching has been simultaneously challenging and rewarding. Taking on an ominous structure like the educational system is not an easy task, but in this struggle I have made lifetime friends, because I'm not alone. It has required a balance in strategy from resistance, to education, social and political action, and finally an exciting phase of development work as Indigenous people world wide create and participate in shaping their own future. It has been, and continues to be, exciting work.

While I was director of the Saskatchewan Urban Native Teacher Education Program, I finally warmed up to the idea of having my own family, inspired by many of my students who were having families while they were studying. Parenting is the most difficult work I have done to date. The passing on of culture, in particular the values to frame your children's own life experiences, cannot be short-changed. Today, children are inundated with many confusing images and messages. I think it is even more important to take our children with us everywhere we go, to develop a relationship with them and to model for them the choices they need to make. Assisting me in preparation for a keynote address, my mother told me once that teaching our children what we know to be important to their lives was truly an act of love, and without it our children would not grow strong. I believe her.

A career in education with the specific interests I have and am committed to has created many opportunities. After fifteen years as an executive assistant in professional development with the Saskatchewan Teachers' Federation in Professional Development, I continue to enjoy the work I do with and for teachers. I also continue to be open to the influence of others on my life, whether it is through their life experiences, struggles or ideas. I am thankful to a great teacher, the late Dr. Mahood, who introduced me to the work of Paulo Freire and other critical readings. When I read *Pedagogy of the Oppressed* (1971) I remember thinking "This person speaks my language and gives me hope." He claimed that the purpose of education was to illuminate reality and to unmask the system of domination that kept us oppressed. His ideas liberated people and landed him in jail. So, ideas can be dangerous to the status quo.

Our ultimate challenge is to reach out to the human family to address the issues that are of common concern to all of us; one of those issues is the politics and ethics of our natural environment. I believe that establishing relationship in a way that goes beyond a person's cultural community is important. Therefore, my goal is to work side by side with others of like mind, to influence thinking and being so that it "honors all life."

Angela: I grew up in a drab urban environment, in a neighborhood whose street names attempted to evoke the surrounding countryside: Heathfield Road, Wildcroft Avenue, Gorseway. Our tiny patch of front garden was planted with standard roses as formal as those at Versailles, while alternate clumps of blue lobelia and white alyssum crouched in an orderly line atop the unforgiving red clay soil of the British Midlands. My early years were circumscribed by the urban environment, but I lived in a neighborhood with very few intruding cars and many back gardens in which we could play. The row houses along Gorseway were immensely respectable, lace curtains kept tidily closed by the wives of workers employed in booming car factories. From 32 Gorseway I ventured out to secondary school across the city, where I first encountered daughters of educated professionals, who had actually eaten in restaurants and travelled outside England. I loved Barr's Hill Grammar School. The bookishness that made me an oddity in my neighborhood was prized at school, where eventually I won the restrained approbation of some of my teachers. Not all my school experiences were happy ones; my parents were advised to send me to elocution lessons, so my local Midland accent could be replaced by something more "cultured." It was only when I went to secondary school that I realized I was a member of the British working class. My mother, who was thrilled that I had "passed the 11 plus exam" that led to entrance to a prestigious grammar school, felt inadequate every time she had to come to my school for an open house or report card meeting. I was agonized by her pallor and shaking hands as she talked with my teachers.

On the advice of my English teacher, at the end of my secondary schooling I applied to a small women's college at the University of London. During my undergraduate years during the 1960s, this college still had a butler, whose job it was to make sure that the "young ladies" were properly attired for dinner. I had inadvertently enrolled myself in an institution that was another relic of the Victorian era. I rebelled more overtly this time, and took on the persona of a dilettante, involved in music and theatre activities, and dressed in black whenever possible. Despite my attempts to be unconventional, I met and married my husband, who delighted my mother because of his "safe" profession.

With my teacher-husband, I emigrated to Canada, where we found ourselves in a small Aboriginal community in British

Columbia. It was a beautiful mountain environment, blessed with salmon-rich rivers and abundant game. Most days were sunny, and a cleansing wind frequently blew through the converging valleys that gave the community its Aboriginal name. There we raised our three children, and encountered for the first time the effects of colonization on Aboriginal people. I loved teaching there, and grew close to many children and families. I played the organ at funerals and cried with families who lost teenagers to violence and alcohol, and I rejoiced when babies were born.

My current life in Saskatchewan reflects many of my earlier experiences. I continue to work with Aboriginal people. I have recently travelled to meet with teachers in the Arctic, as well as in Haida Gwaii. I am also part of a project with Kazak teachers, the Indigenous inhabitants of Kazakstan, supporting them in their struggle to reduce the effects of Russian domination on their education system, and trying hard not to impose yet another world view on their teaching lives. In the more mundane aspects of my life as a professor of education, I teach undergraduate and graduate classes in language arts. I gently prod mainstream pre-service teachers into reflecting on their own privilege as white colonizers of a rich land. Some of my graduate students are Aboriginal, and I am proud to support them in their struggles to reconcile their traditional knowledge with Western academic discourses. I also have Aboriginal colleagues, who are diverse in their interests and backgrounds, and who sometimes tire of educating their peers as well as their students. I continue to work through my life as a teacher educator and researcher to fulfill, even on a small scale, my vision of egalitarian scholarship in the service of social justice.

So now, again, I live in the city, but its effects on my life are mitigated by the ever-present sunshine, the urban forest, and the space between my house and others. I no longer live in a row house, where the smell of next door's food permeated our living room. Now, as part of the middle class, I enjoy comfort and beauty in my everyday life. So I need to remind myself of my roots, and of my early awakening to the divisions between people caused by class and economic inequality. As an academic, I am still plagued by the "impostor syndrome," that sense that one day someone will unmask this working class woman as a fraud, someone who should never have achieved a Ph.D., and is an anomaly in the academy. The College of Education is low in the university hierarchy, perhaps because we attempt to match research and practice, and prepare our students for a profession. We are often treated as interlopers in the system, as "teachers with Ph.D.s," a phrase I once heard used in a pejorative sense. I gladly embrace the phrase as a descriptor of how I see myself.

The Conversation Begins

We recorded and transcribed several conversations, then passed them from one to another for revision. Rita was struck by the number of questions Angela asked, and wondered aloud if it indicated her dominance in the discourse. This is a fair comment, although there may be other explanations. There have been few studies of women talking together, but studies of mixed conversations (for example, Coates and Cameron, 1988) show women using questions as a device to keep the conversation going, and to include all group members. In our conversation, Angela felt she needed to draw on Rita's knowledge as a Métis woman currently living in the city. Nevertheless, Angela would also honestly say that she felt a responsibility to "guide" the discussion so that our linear list of issues was covered. So there is some cultural difference in our discourse management strategies, but the final version of our conversation, combining as it does spoken and written collaboration, enables the reader to hear both voices.

Experiences at School

Angela: As I read our stories, I notice the commonalities and differences that have brought us together at this stage of our lives. Despite difficulties, we were both successful within the school system. I think I expected secondary school to be easy because I did not think of myself as being from a different culture than that of the school. The reality was that I was from a different subculture, though of course in my neighborhood we all shared similar incomes and similar backgrounds. It was only when I went to secondary school, which involved my travelling out of the neighborhood, that suddenly I realized that there were people in the world who were very different from me, and that they had different access to the world than I had. My sense was that I was regarded as inferior because I had not had those same experiences. It was a very rude awakening.

Rita: The most difficult challenge for me was not school itself or learning the English language. I must admit though, the more subtle aspects of conversing in English gave me some difficulty. It was hard trying to understand what people really meant sometimes. An aspect of the English language that was very difficult to grasp, for example, was the use of idiomatic expressions. To this day, I have difficulty with idioms. Often, I take the expressions literally. My attempts to use idioms in everyday speech is a form of entertainment for people around me. Overall though, I loved school.

Angela: I loved to read and I loved books and learning Latin and Greek. My family had some of the same responses to my education as your grandfather had to yours. They wondered if I went away, and had all this education, would I come back to the community? My mother, I think, always knew that I wouldn't come back, but I didn't realize until quite recently that she recognized this. So there was always an ambivalence at home about the fact that I was successful at school.

Rita: I don't know if my grandfather wanted me to return home, necessarily; what was important was that I did not forget the important values I had been taught, values that were important for my well being. Learning, and particularly thinking, in English sometimes created a conflict. I remember one incident vividly. Whenever I would return home for a visit during school breaks, my grandfather would remind me of the importance of paying respect to all the old people when I had arrived. In Cree, he referred to them as my grandmothers and grandfathers. On one occasion, I decided to correct him, telling him that the old people in the community were not my grandmothers and grandfathers as he had suggested. Further, my cousin Linda was not my sister as he often referenced her in relation to me.

Angela: So you had taken on the white discourse.

Rita: Yes, I had taken it on, big time. I was learning the language and the culture and accepting it as the truth. Imagine correcting your grandfather!

Issues of Language and Dialect

Angela: The language carries important information about the culture. So maintaining Indigenous languages is very important. How do you maintain your own language now?

Rita: Only through speaking with my extended family. It was the only means of communicating with an aunt who raised me and passed away this Spring. Michif was her primary language. I also maintain contact with my mom once a week, and we often converse in Cree/Michif. During my sabbatical about five years ago, I ran cross country with a Cree speaker from Alberta. During our runs, we spoke Cree. She has become a good friend and whenever we have an opportunity to converse in Cree we do so. It isn't as polished as when I have been immersed for a few days in the language.

Angela: There's a deep comfort, isn't there, when you can do that. I know when I went back just a couple of years ago to the street in the Midlands of England where I was raised, I visited the women who were there when I grew up. It's not a transient neighborhood at all. I slid back into my Midland accent very easily. There are some interesting parallels with your experiences, because we used to call all the women on our street Auntie, though they weren't related to me by blood as were the people in your home community. Nevertheless, because we had grown up together, we used "Auntie" as a kind of courtesy title. It meant that we really could go to those houses if our mom wasn't there, and we knew we would be looked after. I still get letters from a couple of the older women there; they tell me who has died recently: "Oh, old Mrs. Goodwin went, you know, she had been having a hard time with her legs." But there is a sense of comfort when you're back in that environment, you don't have to think about how to respond. I know how to do it because it was very much a part of me. But it's very different from the way I am in other places.

Rita: So, as long as your culture and language is respected and held up as it was in my community, learning another language and culture is not necessarily negative, assuming all things are equal. This hasn't been the case for Aboriginal people in Canada, or for that matter for Indigenous people world wide. It was when I left my community that I really began to feel my difference. It was brought to my attention subtly through the curriculum by the ways in which Aboriginal history and experiences were treated. I would also be singled out to explain things. When you live in a culture, you just live it, you don't know the qualities of it, you're not studying it, per se.

Angela: You can understand why teachers do that, though. It's tempting to call on people as possible representatives of a culture that you yourself haven't experienced. But of course that person is put into an untenable position, having to speak for everyone. In this situation students are made to feel outside the mainstream.

Did you ever feel on the outside of your own community, or did you feel that you could re-enter – that it was fine to be able to do that?

Rita: No, I think we were viewed with some suspicion from our own communities, initially. It took a long time for me to understand why. It's because you may be bringing in ideas that run counter to the ideas that the community values. The consumption of "Western culture" through mass media is probably more detrimental to our languages and cultures today. Most of the education we receive in public school and university is about the culture outside of our communities. If individuals don't question it or build from the foundation of the early education they received, assuming they were fortunate enough to have that opportunity, then it's possible that they will assume values that are not congruent with the home community. Then, you can quickly run amok in your own community. Whenever I return home to visit, I go as a participant; I would never suggest I know better or more. I think the caution that my late grandfather provided has helped me.

Identity Across Cultural and Racial Boundaries

Angela: Your reality is experienced by many people described in the book. They are trying to work out how they fit with their communities, but they haven't lived to the life stage that you have. In some cases, they don't know what their identity is and they don't recognize what's happening to them. Shauneen Pete-Willett knows where she fits and uses the story of Coyote to show where that place is. The whole book is about the constraints brought to bear on people and how those constraints force them to examine who they are. Those who are successfully able to reflect on their own culture and its relationship to the Eurocentric mainstream are often the ones who have had more education. They have learned to step across cultural and racial boundaries and to examine their own values. But for those who are still learning, it's a very uncomfortable place. I'm wondering if the young people whose stories are told in the first section of the book have a home community that they can visit. Establishing identities in urban communities where there is such diversity is a challenge for young Aboriginal people.

Diversity Within the Urban Aboriginal Population

Rita: We all have very different experiences as Aborginal people, that's part of the challenge. To make this point, at a recent conference, three of us Métis women shared what was common and different about our experiences. One of us was raised in an urban environment, with some family members ashamed to say who they are to this very day. Another grew up in a small urban community, and described how racial difference played itself out in her family. Family members who were fair-skinned didn't have as much difficulty in the schools as she did, because she was the dark one in her family. Her own community appeared to hold to the same views as the larger community. Of course, I grew up in Ile-a-la-Crosse, in what I would describe as a closely knit Métis community. What binds us as Aboriginal women, as Métis women, is a colonial history which resulted from the dispossession of land, vital to our economic well-being and our identity as a people. So, coming back to the voices in the book, remember Shannon in Carol Leroy's chapter? She has assumed a stereotype of "Indianness" as exhibiting toughness and concludes that because she is fair skinned she can't be "Indian." It would be interesting to know how resolved the issues are within her own immediate family. I'm guessing they are probably not resolved. This is amplified by prevailing negative stereotypes and static, essentialist notions of identity, which contribute to her confusion.

Educators' Responses to Diversity

Angela: We have talked about the way the complexity of all these social issues plays out in children's lives. Rita, your question was, are educators aware of these complexities? I know that one of my responses is that we need to encourage teachers to develop a critical, almost ethnographic eye. I speak from that perspective because I have been involved in action research with teachers, both Aboriginal and non-Aboriginal. This research encourages participants to look at the educational system from both insider and outsider perspectives.

Rita: I recognize that sometimes it's probably easier to move away from these issues because they are controversial and unresolved in the larger community. Yet the stories in the book would say to us that we need to address the oppressive conditions of poverty and racism. As educators, we need to help students deconstruct various kinds of oppression to support their understanding of them, for the purposes of assisting their own personal growth.

Angela: Is deconstructing and understanding enough, or should we then move onto action? Can we say to children, "Well this is the way the world works; you're oppressed or you're the oppressor, because historically these things have happened?" Do we go beyond that to say we need to protest it in some way? Or do we simply need to understand?

Rita: Well, first of all I don't think any purpose is served in blaming. Protest? I'm not sure. Perhaps. I think the purpose is to understand the systemic nature of the issues. Yes, I think understanding is the beginning point. Hopefully, this kind of education will support holistic growth of individuals so they can be contributing members of society. Public education has a role in advocating learning for social justice. To do this, one must begin with the experiences of the students. I think educators also need to imagine the future with their students. When teachers create such opportunities, young people are given opportunity to respond in positive ways. Bente Huntley's chapter speaks to this issue of building onto the concerns of the students.

Angela: Sometimes a project on the environment may be carried out in schools, but it usually doesn't involve the children giving up anything or changing anything that they're doing. It's an attractive thing for middle class kids to do. We're "saving the world" but still having two showers a day or buying food that's shrink-wrapped or whatever. Part of me worries about schools taking these things on and turning them into romantic crusades.

Rita: I share your concern.

Integrating Aboriginal Perspectives and Content into Curriculum

Rita: On another topic, last night I was with a friend who wanted me to react to a unit of work on Aboriginal peoples that was being proposed by a teacher. The whole focus was on crafts, such as making a canoe or making a tipi. It's too easy for the inclusion of Indian and Métis perspectives in a curriculum to degenerate into a series of activities that don't amount to anything. The work that Joe Duquette High School does in Saskatoon, Saskatchewan, and the work that the Saskatchewan Urban Native Teacher Education Program does, give us excellent models of what it means to "integrate Aboriginal content and perspectives." For example, both use drama with the students as a way to explore what is happening in students' lives. I've heard students graduating from these programs talk about how liberating that experience was for them because it helped them think about important issues for themselves. Many of those stories help students imagine ways to create a different future for themselves.

Angela: That's why the sections in the book that describe these programs move me very much. Drama keeps us busy, if you like, but it keeps us busy with reflection and action. Many teachers are reluctant to do drama because it doesn't feel comfortable.

Rita: I can appreciate the difficulty of positioning curriculum to meet the diversity of student needs. Alternative programs may be the most viable and efficient structure to deliver the curriculum to students with particular needs. In innovative programs the teacher provides a vehicle for students to bring the variety of their experience to the learning process. Each of them can bring their own understandings and challenges, as they do at SUNTEP. The students then make meaning of their lives collectively. The teacher is there to guide and provide those opportunities. The crafts focus I described earlier is superficial and doesn't tell you anything about Aboriginal people. All it does is reinforce more stereotypes. A higher quality of integration of Indian and Métis perspectives is realized when teachers legitimize Indigenous knowledge, history and experience throughout the curriculum.

Angela: To do what you have described, you need a range of knowledge. This would mean that the teacher has a background in Aboriginal studies, and is not just reading information to prepare for this one unit. That's much more to ask of teachers than to have them prepare a unit on Aboriginal legends. I think there are parallels with people who teach music in the school and don't play an instrument, don't sing, so have to fall back onto a commercial music program. It's very difficult to prepare teachers to integrate Aboriginal content and perspectives without giving them a foundational knowledge of Aboriginal history and culture. But I really worry that we don't typically train our teachers this way. Our students in education are very busy doing courses and writing assignments. They really aren't given time in the program to read and think about the world, or to follow their own interests and build up the kind of knowledge that they could integrate when they're planning their programs.

Rita: Any topic teachers don't feel conversant with through a broad sense of history would probably lead them to teach history as facts and chronology rather than something that's much more living and rich.

Angela: The challenge of integrating Indian and Métis content is also pertinent for some Aboriginal teachers who may not have grown up immersed in the culture. Recently qualified teachers have probably had cross-cultural courses as part of their teacher education, but even so, there are limits to that.

My other question is about how to describe Indian and Métis content? What is it that we want to integrate?

Rita: It is taking into account Aboriginal people's experiences, as I have said earlier, and whether that's historical or cultural, it doesn't matter. Aboriginal history is the history of this country. It's part of your history, Angela, now that you are a citizen of this country. According to history textbooks, the relationship between the newcomers and the Indigenous people seems to have stopped after the arrival of the British and French. I don't believe it stopped, because the tensions remain and the relationship is unresolved. The history of Aboriginal people is not woven or intertwined with the history of this country. That's what I think the integration of Aboriginal people's experience and history is all about; it's integrating it into the fabric of what we call Canadian history, Canadian art, and Canadian literature and other subject areas.

Angela: I was quite taken aback that when my family came here from England and our children didn't get an opportunity to be bilingual in French and English. Now I wonder if the day will come when it will be required that my grandchildren will learn an Aboriginal language in the Canadian school system. If we required that everyone had to learn an Aboriginal language, would it make a difference?

Rita: I think that would be a long haul, unfortunately, because there would be resistance. You would have to break down the stereotype that Indigenous languages do not have the same sophistication as the English language. From a pragmatic point of view, there is also the issue of loss of speakers. The Maori in New Zealand have made excellent strides in the revival and use of their language, but I know they have had a challenge in meeting the demand for fluent speakers to carry their programs. Fluency means people who can speak the language and write in the language.

I think that Aboriginal knowledge and world views should be given value in our school system. What we are doing now is piecemeal. What separates Aboriginal history from Canadian history? If we are interested in seeking knowledge, for example, on conceptions of community, why would we reject or be afraid of exploring an Indigenous perspective on this idea?

Angela: In the nineteenth century people used to take the grand tour in Europe as part of their education. The idea was that you would visit other cultures and come back intellectually and culturally richer. The more you knew about another culture, the more educated you were. Unfortunately, it only applied to some cultures. Perhaps our young people should spend the time between high school and post-secondary education exploring different regional and cultural perspectives within their own country. Canadians could learn more about Aboriginal cultures this way.

Rita: I think that another way to integrate Aboriginal perspectives into schools is by using literature and myths or legends, stories that Indigenous people tell to explain the natural world, like the constellations of stars, for example. The stories contain scientific knowledge and community values. You learn the proper relationships between men and women, or the proper relationships between a mother and a son, granted from an Indigenous perspective. This is true of contemporary stories that Indigenous people write. A teacher with little background knowledge and experience with Aboriginal people could use these if they wanted to integrate Indigenous knowledge. They can learn along with their students.

Angela: Trickster stories, which are common in most cultures, also teach us about community values, because the trickster is always pushing the boundaries of appropriate behavior. The trickster's behavior is right at the boundary where you see what is acceptable or not. The trickster is a wonderful character from an ethnographic point of view, because again, being on the margins he just sees the world a little differently than the community and brings a particular sort of wisdom.

Addressing Spirituality in the Schools

Angela: I know that teachers get very concerned about being asked to talk about topics that address spirituality within a culture. How do you respond to teachers who say, "Well I'm not sure, I'd better ask, I can't do this, I'm going to ask an Aboriginal person or I'm not going to do anything?"

Rita: Shauneen's story raises this issue. The concern about certain ceremonies being used in schools has been raised a number of times. Smudging and rituals are being considered by parents and communities as religious or presenting a certain way of worship. As if the Lord's Prayer is not religious! To treat this issue seriously, I would probably be uncertain in my own response to a question such as this from teachers. The goals of education include spiritual development, and the curriculum provides the opportunity to study different religions. However, public schools cannot push one religion over another. People express their spirituality in different ways, which don't always translate into religion, but they could do so. It is an extremely controversial and sensitive area, isn't it? I suppose as with all controversial issues, teachers need to be sensitive and work with community leaders on these issues. I think human spirituality is worthy of study. I don't believe that schools should espouse particular religions and belief systems. If a community expresses the need for offering a spiritual program, I think there must always be a choice for individuals (both students and teachers) to opt out. It isn't safe either to assume that Aboriginal peoples are homogeneous in their practices and expressions of spirituality. I have heard some school board members say that you can't push the integration of Indian and Métis content on people because there's going to be a backlash. The claim is that, if they do this for the Aboriginal culture, members of "other" cultures will be offended. This response is a way of "othering" some cultures and not perceiving the mainstream as a culture, or not seeing that "white" is a color. Our challenge as educators is really ethnocentrism.

But I would also extend the discussion to include other topics; ethnocentrism isn't mitigated only by the integration of Indian and Métis content into curriculum. I think we need to consider all the equity-related policies of the province, including multiculturalism, gender equity and class issues. As we've read the stories in the chapters for this book, all these issues come into play. Understanding the critical theory of race, class and gender issues is one way to support teachers' learning. It is the responsibility of teacher education programs to introduce pre-service teachers to these critical issues, and the role of education systems to develop programs which resist current societal inequities.

Alternative Education Programs

Rita: There are some hopeful signs for urban education in the alternative education programs mentioned in the book. It's quite clear that these programs move away from the rigid notion of knowledge as something that you transmit in a pencil and paper kind of way. The commonality in the programs described in the book is the emphasis on students' engagement, not just in activity, but in reflection. It's a combination of looking deep into one's own experience, drawing on that and then doing something that's active and expressive versus trying to discover others' knowledge and writing it down or regurgitating it in some kind of way.

Alternative programs also attract educators who are much more willing to put themselves at risk. They want to make a difference in the lives of their students. I think of Parker Palmer's book *The Courage to Teach* (1998) and Herbert Kohl's newest book, *Discipline of Hope* (1998). Teachers can and do make a difference when they bring their whole selves to the act of teaching.

Angela: This view of teaching also relates to Nel Noddings' (1984) notion of relational knowing and seeing yourself first in relation to the students. The people who are ready to do that are more likely to teach in a very different way and can see knowledge as constructed together, for instance. I'm thinking too, of Arlene Stairs' work (1995) where she talks about two different Inuit labels for learning and teaching. She talks about the kind of knowledge that you learn by being with someone and then the knowledge that you learn at school as different. Perhaps what alternative schools do, is put those types of knowledge together in integrated ways.

Rita: It is not just the content, and the fact that probably their curriculum reflects in a visible way Aboriginal history, perspectives and world views. I think it's deeper than that. I think the teachers care. It's not easy to work in those programs if you're a beginning teacher because you still feel the constraints of an imposed curriculum. Teachers may also feel pressured to transmit a body of knowledge that can seem societally important for students to know. Still, the biased information in books transmitted as a "body of knowledge" can be responsible for the carnage, the subtle damage, done to you as an Aboriginal person. Knowledge is always happening outside you. It's constructed by others but never with you, or within your own community. It's important to understand that we can build knowledge through our own experience; that this everyday knowledge is valued in our lives. I think people used to call it wisdom or a form of spiritual knowledge. Alternative education programs recognize the importance of factual and propositional knowledge, as well as the crucial relationship between teacher and student, but the best of these programs also bring an underlying critical element to the curriculum, which acknowledges class and race issues. If these class and race issues are not recognized and named, students may spend their school lives resisting both curriculum content and their teachers. It also respects different ways of knowing, different world views.

Angela: Ogbu (1991) discusses secondary cultural differences that are built in resistance to the mainstream way of doing things. Sometimes the way that resistance is manifested is more harmful to the person who is manifesting the resistance than it is to the system itself. That's a horrible irony. There aren't really very many ways to resist, especially if you're a child or a young person. Those kinds of resistance that are maintained, often generation to generation in the city, are often counterproductive.

Rita: I agree. However, in a context of unequal access to power, some types of resistance are healthy and productive. Framing history and experiences from your own point of view in a story is an example. While missionaries may have told one story in their reports back to the bishop, or the Hudson's Bay Company factors may have written into their journals biased accounts of the good work they had carried out on behalf of their company, another version was circulating in the Aboriginal community. This version of events turns the tables so that the heroes are people in your own community. I heard many stories like this growing up as a child. The context hasn't changed much; as an affirmation, my friends and I continue the tradition of centring our own experience. A story such as this is often told with humor. I don't see that form of resistance as harmful because it's a way of preserving who you are; it's a recognition that there is a power imbalance. I grew up with this tradition and I see it as a very healthy form of resistance.

When we were kids, my late grandfather would take my cousins and me through the graveyard for walks and what he told us about the priests and sisters laid to rest in a cordoned-off section of the graveyard was quite blasphemous. All the while our grandmother would be scolding him. She provided the balance. I loved his blasphemy and I think my cousins did too.

I experienced working class solidarity in the fun that you would make of people in the upper classes, whom we considered to be effete and impractical. So that was one way of resistance. I think silence is another form of powerful resistance, where rather than engage in a disrespectful interaction, nothing is given. Yes, there are harmful responses. Herbert Kohl (1994) addresses this important topic in, "I Won't Learn From You: The Role of Assent in Learning." As educators, we need to understand that resistance is sometimes a desperate measure to maintain dignity and control. Heather Blair describes the students in her study as constructing shifting and intersecting countercultures in opposition to the school system, but also to each other.

Colonization

Rita: My exploration of the literature on colonization, race, class and gender issues sometimes suggests a hierarchy of oppression, but I am not sure it serves any purpose. If you look at an issue only from a particular frame of reference, or for example, you make gender the only issue, you may forget about class or race. In the case of Indigenous people, historical context and the process of colonization are also very important considerations.

Razack in her book *Looking White People in the Eye: Gender, Race and Culture in Courtrooms and Classrooms* (1998), creates a complex and multi-faceted landscape as she attempts to address concerns for equity and social justice. There is a social context, a historical context and often a political context. The factors contributing to inequity and injustice are many. They often intersect with one another and, according to Razack (1998), a deeper analysis of these interlocking oppressions might lead us to the discovery of our own complicity. One's first response is "No, not me." Because of my education, I am at an income level that would make me middle class. While I resist anything that smacks of upper class in my own home, like a spare set of dishes and a living room that is not meant for everyday use, I am middle class, nonetheless. Does what I am accustomed to and expect create hardship for people who have less than me? Does my position contribute to inequity down the line?

We have to believe in the possibility that systemic inequities can be resolved at a number of levels in North American society. The Royal Commission on Aboriginal People points the hope to a renewed look at the relationship between Canadians and Aboriginal peoples. It takes more than one group to do that, and it's difficult to reconcile any relationship so long as it's unequal. The relationship between Aboriginal communities and Canada remains unequal in terms of political and economic power.

Angela: Looking historically across the world, are there examples of countries that have ever renegotiated the relationship between colonizers and colonized groups? All the examples that I can think of have tended to simply wait long enough for assimilation, in Europe for instance.

Rita: What I've observed in my trips to Geneva as a participant in the discussions of the Working Group of Indigenous Peoples is that on the surface the so-called developed countries, as opposed to developing countries, often report more success in terms of negotiating a new or better relationship, but when I step back, really far, far back, I don't know of any who have achieved a relationship that's based on mutual respect. I could say more, but I won't at this time.

Angela: We know in the urban environment we're going to have increasing numbers of Aboriginal people. There is an immediate need to consider issues of the power and balance between Aboriginal and non-Aboriginal peoples in cities. So if we start from that premise then, that we're doing the work in a context that is not neutral, and we understand that there is an imbalance of power, can we work from there to create some of the solutions? As teachers we need to look beyond the immediate world of the classroom to unequal relationships in the broader society which are reflected in schools. But it's more comfortable as an educator to say "Well, we need to be providing at the classroom level for content that matches experience in the children that we're teaching, and to treat people with respect with whatever background they're from." What's important is that we acknowledge that that's never enough. It should be done, but it's not sufficient.

Rita: Alternative programs are a short-term response that doesn't change the larger picture, but they create opportunities for individual students to succeed. Alternative programs acknowledge the reality that exists, rather than espousing liberal mainstream notions of we're all equal here and we all have a place. Returning to Razack's (1998) work, in the context of unequal power, she invites her readers to examine themselves within the social hierarchies around them. She states "We need to ask: Where am I in this picture? Am I positioning myself as the saviour of less fortunate people? As the progressive one? As more subordinated? As innocent?" (p. 170). She claims these are moves of superiority and we need to move beyond them.

Angela: How do we position ourselves? We have different responsibilities in the educational community. I think for me one of the things that has happened is that I've often been reluctant to accept the power that's come with the position that I have, and I've tended to think of myself still as a poor working class person, although in fact I have a great deal of power and influence on a number of people. The responsibility that goes with that can be very

188 Resting Lightly on Mother Earth

uncomfortable. There were lots of years where I did see myself, not as a savior, but probably as the "progressive person" with something to offer, but perhaps always thinking that I had solidarity with Aboriginal people because of my own experiences. They're not always comfortable reflections are they?

Rita: No, no, they're not. I have assumed a great deal of responsibility from the beginning. I have seen myself as an advocate for Aboriginal students and Aboriginal peoples. As much as I have not wanted to be viewed as a representative of my community, I am. As an educator who is Aboriginal, I have assumed a stance that I belong here. I see myself as a member of various communities trying to make a difference. I have also recognized that I have achieved success because of the support I received from my family, and indirectly, my community. I feel very fortunate, but I also worked hard, in every sense of the word, to be here today. Like many of the voices we heard, I have a need to reconnect with my own family/community from time to time. My uncle and I had this wonderful conversation the other day about coming home. I was sharing with him stories of my work, my fatigue, and my struggles. He said, "Well, maybe you should come home," and I said, "Well, I think spiritually I need to come home, and I'm on that journey, but I know I can't come home physically." He said, "You play an important role from where you are." It was important for me to hear that, because I still need reassurance I am on the right track and I need to feel that I'm connected.

It's the kind of connection that participants in the last chapter of the book talk about, going backwards and forwards and renewing themselves in different contexts.

The Evolution of Identity and Language

Rita: The notion of positionality is intimately connected with how we construct identities in the cultures and subcultures in which we live. So long as identity is viewed as static or is essentialized, I will never be able to reconcile who I am. I was born in 1950, which puts me in a historical social context that is different from the generation before me, and so what I have had to do to survive economically, culturally, spiritually and socially, my grandfather could never have fully imagined. The idea of change naturally causes anxiety in many communities, especially language change. It happens to English, it happens to all languages.

If there's something important in a language that needs to be kept, people will keep it. The same is true for cultural identity. If there are characteristics that are really resilient, that are powerful, that enable you to function well in the world and in many different ways, those aren't going to change. Those connections stay. I think where cultural identity is at risk it is for people who are not sure who they are, and who perhaps are in very stressful circumstances where they have cause to question their natural response all the time. As Indigenous people, we contribute to reinforcing the notion of a static cultural identity ourselves without recognizing that it's happening. We need to challenge that, because our identities have evolved as our languages have. There is a strong connection between language and identity, but not to the extent that we would say that anyone who has lost their language is not Aboriginal.

Having said that, we need to create institutions that nurture Indigenous languages and their continued development because I believe that our identity as Indigenous people begins and resides in the languages. That's how I would frame the importance of identity with Indigenous languages; that's where my identity begins. If we are going to celebrate that part of who we are, we need institutions to focus on this important resource so further generations have opportunity to study it or to study in the language. Willie Ermine in "Pedagogy From the Ethos: An Interview with Elder Ermine on Language" (Stiffarm, 1998) states that it's the language that holds the ethos of how it is we are supposed to be with each other, and how we're supposed to be with the land. The language holds all that information and so that's why you should nurture and preserve Aboriginal languages. What I have said does not negate the necessity of learning to speak English.

My grandfather wanted me to learn the English language, but not to forget my own. That's the accident or opportunity that was afforded by cultures coming together. I think my grandfather must have understood already how the world was organized and he knew that I had to understand the English language to survive.

Land and Spirituality

Rita: Being able to understand what is being said in English and Cree is one thing; trying to reconcile ideas and the concepts based on two, often opposing, world views is very difficult. This brings us back to the issue of land. References to land in the English language are often disconnected from people. References are objectified and commodified. In Cree, concepts and ideas of land are often personified and active, or in flux. So what do you do when you can't reconcile the concepts in the two languages? Are they separate, parallel ways of thinking? Sometimes I watch my own son; it seems that the world he lives in is machines and images, and unless I tell him to look at the sky, I don't know if he notices it.

Angela: Cajete (1999) describes this phenomenon of disconnection from the natural world: "As we change our landscapes and allow the self-serving will of materialist economic systems to have sway over our view of the land, we also allow the natural landscape of mind and soul to be altered in the same measure" (p. 18). How do we reconnect children with an understanding of their place in the world? That's an enormous question. Does it happen through the kinds of approaches we're talking about in alternative education programs? It seems to me that's not going far enough. It's just slightly different from what's happening in the mainstream.

There are alternative views of our place in the world, which resonate with Indigenous traditions. Glanzberg (1999) suggests that it is possible for human beings to live in harmony with the natural world by adopting the principles of perma-culture that "By observing nature we can learn to imitate and work with the features of the landscape and all living things to provide for our own needs, rather than working against natural systems" (p. 227). The premise seems to be that we begin to know by learning about the environment in which we live in and by understanding the foundational principles which include inter-relatedness. But if we provide students with an education that is disconnected from the land and natural principles, we create a skewed reality. The hopeful message, according to Glanzberg (1999), is that "When humans understand that everything around them is alive, and that it is sacred, nothing is trivial." This appreciation of unconstrained interrelationship is a tremendous responsibility, but also a blessing. "Human actions are no longer small and meaningless, but important and powerful" (p. 239).

References

Cajete, G. 1999. " 'Look to the Mountain': Reflections on Indigenous Ecology." In *A People's Ecology: Explorations in Sustainable Living*, edited by G. Cajete, pp. 3-20. Santa Fe: Clear Light Publishers.

Canada. 1996. Royal Commission on Aboriginal Peoples. Ottawa: Minister of Supply and Services, Canada.

Coates, J. and Cameron, D., eds. 1988. *Women in Their Speech Communities*. London: Longman.

Ermine, W. 1998. "Pedagogy from the Ethos: An Interview with Elder Ermine on Language." In *As We See...: Aboriginal Pedagogy*, edited by Lenore Stiffarm. Saskatoon, SK: University Extension Press, University of Saskatchewan.

Freire, P. 1971. *Pedagogy of the Oppressed*. New York: Seaview.

Glanzberg, J. 1999. "Permaculture as a Way of Seeing and Acting in the World." In *A People's Ecology: Explorations in Sustainable Living*, edited by G. Cajete, pp. 227-42. Santa Fe: Clear Light Publishers.

Kohl, H. 1994. *"I Won't Learn from You" and Other Thoughts on Creative Maladjustment*. New York: The New Press.

Noddings, N. 1984. *Caring: A Feminine Approach to Ethics and Moral Education*. Berkeley, CA: University of California Press.

Ogbu, J. 1991. "Immigrant and Non-voluntary Minorities in Comparative Perspective." In *Minority Status and Schooling*, edited by M. Gibson and J. Ogbu. New York: Garland Publishing.

Palmer, P. 1998. *The Courage to Teach*. San Francisco, CA: Jossey-Bass Publishers.

Razack, S. 1998. *Looking White People in the Eye*. Toronto: University of Toronto Press.

Stairs, A. 1995. "Learning and Teaching in Native Education." In *The Circle Unfolds: First Nations Education in Canada*, edited by M. Battiste and J. Barman. Vancouver, BC: University of British Columbia Press.

Information about Contributors

Heather Blair is an Associate Professor in Elementary Education at the University of Alberta. Heather has worked in Aboriginal Education, nationally and internationally, for the past 20 years. She is interested in the intersections of race, class, ethnicity and gender for early adolescents in Canadian schools.

Lon Borgerson teaches drama and writing at the Saskatchewan Urban Native Teacher Education Program and directs SUNTEP Theatre. His co-authors are students and graduates of SUNTEP-Prince Albert.

Rita Bouvier currently serves as an executive assistant in Professional Development with the Saskatchewan Teachers Federation. She works with, and on behalf of teachers to promote teacher voice on all matters affecting teaching and learning, and to provide leadership on issues affecting public education. Her professional and research interests are cultural and systemic issues affecting teaching and learning.

Bente Huntley has a diploma in Renewable Resources Technology from Kelsey Institute, a B.Ed. from SUNTEP Prince Albert and a Masters Degree with the Department of Curriculum Studies, College of Education at the University of Saskatchewan. Because of her interest in plants and stories (passed on from her grandparents), Bente completed her M.Ed. project on Traditional Environmental Knowledge of the Cree People of North-Central Saskatchewan. In addition, Bente has recently completed the "Science and Culture Nexus Research Project" with Dr. Glen Aikenhead from the University of Saskatchewan. Bente currently teaches Native Studies and the science methods classes for SUNTEP, Prince Albert.

Dorothy F. King is currently associate professor of education at Westminster College in Missouri. She has spent the last 18 years working with schools in American Indian nations. Through the years, she's co-ordinated many in-service workshops for consortia of schools, bringing together administrators, parents, school board members, teachers, students and nationally recognized facilitators.

Carol Leroy was a classroom teacher in intercultural settings in Canada and Kenya. She is currently an Assistant Professor in the Department of Elementary Education at the University of Alberta, where her teaching and research focuses on the literacy of children in difficulty.

Shauneen Pete-Willett has worked as a teacher and Educational Consultant for eight years. She is presently completing doctoral studies at the Centre for the Study of Higher Education at the University of Arizona. Her research interests include school effectiveness, administrator preparation and the changing nature of faculty work.

Carol Reid is a Lecturer in Cross-cultural studies in the Faculty of Education and Languages at the University of Western Sydney, Australia. She teaches graduate and undergraduate courses on cultural diversity and the sociology of education. She has been involved in research into cultural diversity and inequality in urban settings and her doctorate was a comparative study of Indigenous teacher education in Australia and Canada.

Willard H. Walters is chief executive officer and principal of Gila Crossing Community School in Komatke, AZ, serving Akmiel O'Otham and Peeposh peoples. Under Walter's leadership the school has been nationally recognized for its programs. Walters has been honored for his leadership by both the National Council of Teachers of English and the National Indian School Board Association. He was born and raised on the Cheyenne River Reservation.

Angela Ward was born in England and spent her early years there. She moved to Canada in 1968, and has spent most of her adult life working with Aboriginal peoples in British Columbia and Saskatchewan. She is currently Associate Professor in Curriculum Studies at the University of Saskatchewan.

Linda Wason-Ellam is a professor at the University of Saskatchewan in the Department of Curriculum Studies, where she teaches courses in Literacy, Children's Literature and Qualitative Methodology. She has had extensive experience as a researcher in cross-cultural classrooms in Finland, Inner-city London, Northern Ireland, the US and Canada. She has published many articles that make the social-cultural worlds of children problematic.

Sharon S. Wells is a member of the Choctaw Nation of Oklahoma. For over 27 years Wells has served American Indian children, their families and tribes as a teacher and program administrator at local, regional and national levels. She's been instrumental in helping schools secure funding for innovative programs and services to communities.

AGMV Marquis

MEMBER OF THE SCABRINI GROUP
Quebec, Canada